DEAR ELECTOR

Nesta Wyn Ellis has fought four elections as a Liberal candidate and is a journalist whose pieces have appeared in many newspapers and magazines, including *Punch* and *The Guardian*.

To put this book together she has interviewed a small army of people intimately concerned with the workings of parliament; and has dug deep into the life-styles of the various groups of politicians as they are manifested both within and without the House. The result is a revealing and lively book that will both inform and interest a wide section of people of all political persuasions; and also lead people to ask themselves pertinent questions as to the survival of the parliamentary system as we know it.

Dear Elector
The Truth About MPs

Nesta Wyn Ellis

CORONET BOOKS
Hodder Paperbacks Ltd., London

Printed in Great Britain for
Coronet Books,
Hodder Paperbacks Limited,
St. Paul's House, Warwick Lane,
London EC4P 4AH,
by Cox & Wyman Limited,
London, Reading and Fakenham

ISBN 0 340 18995 9

Acknowledgments

Thanks are due in the preparation of this book to all those who have talked freely over the years about the triumphs and frustrations of their Parliamentary work; also to the Liberal Associations of Spelthorne, Brighton Pavilion and Chipping Barnet for helping to provide me with my own election experience, and to other candidates and political contemporaries in all parties. Special thanks are due to those who assisted directly with the preparation of the manuscript. Captain William Elliott, Reg Underhill and Penny Kinnenmonth who were at the time in charge of candidate selection in the three main parties; David Steel, MP, and his assistant Archie Kirkwood; Marcus Lipton, MP; Brian Walden, MP; Norman Atkinson, MP; Andrew Bowden, MP; Janet Fookes; John and Joy Pardoe and their three children, Rupert, Johnathan and Tania; Mr. and Mrs. Ben Whittaker; John Gorst, MP; Dafydd Wigley, MP; Margot MacDonald; Ian Aitken; Dr. Jeremy Bray; Ernest Roberts, General Secretary, AUEW; Peter Kirk; Will Edwards; Arthur Butler and Lord Avebury. I also want to thank William Davis for his help, encouragement and advice on the manuscript, and Yvonne Mickle who typed it.

To My Parents

Contents

INTRODUCTION

Dear Elector,

If you know anything at all about your Member of Parliament it could be his name. What the Member does when he is not in his constituency or even then is anyone's guess. The occasional quote, the odd appearance on television, a newspaper article, a picture in the local rag, at best a question asked in the House one wet afternoon will be about all that will keep the average MP in your mind.

There are exceptions, Members who become Ministers, Junior Ministers, and even Prime Ministers: there are those that have the knack of hitting the headlines whatever they do or say. But what of the ordinary back-bencher, the man who never says a four letter word in the House or boo to the Speaker, who never gets exposed to the limelight of controversy or the late night TV show: the man who rarely goes in for the ministerial promotional stakes. What makes him tick? How does he spend his time — or yours? And why is he in Parliament at all.

If the job were written up in a careers brochure it might attract even fewer applicants. Its essence is crystallised in the remark of an American lady to her Senator. 'What are you doing about everything' is what most electors would like to ask their MP. The taxpayer has a right to ask but what is the answer? Lloyd George, introducing the first public payment of Members to the House in 1912, referred to the job as 'great and honourable public service', but a taxpayer searching round for signs of service today would be hard pushed to define its nature or to say how that service should be rendered — assuming it is possible to render it at all.

If electors gripe about the 'uselessness' of Parliament they could have a point. The fact that their elected Member is only a cog in the Government or Opposition machine has not escaped

9

them and when the Government of the day rats — as ever — on its hustings vows, it is largely Parliament which gets the blame.

Polling booth disappointment is a recognition of the ineffectiveness of MPs individually to combat the powers of the men and the institutions that run the nation's affairs. As so many electors sourly say 'no one takes any notice of what we think until election time'. Politicians are according to electors, 'all the same' in their disregard of ordinary folk: all they seem to want from their electors is a ticket to Westminster. Once there, MPs, say voters, are only interested in themselves and 'what they can get out of politics'.

Newspapers and the other media serve to reinforce the disgust of the populace for its representatives. On the whole reportage of MPs tends to obscure the serious and the important — and to play up the frivolous behaviour of the debating chamber. Party politics at its most extreme and often most ludicrous is emphasised to the point where people are heard exclaiming that a coalition would be a better way of running the country.

All this is bad for democracy. In recent years the fact that MPs do not have the powers of representation that most electors would hope has become increasingly apparent. Members of Parliament tend therefore to be regarded as rather useless eunuchs, or worse as crooks and deliberate deceivers. As the powers of Government encroach more into everyday life, and MPs seem powerless to act in ordinary people's interest, the disgust has grown. But how fair is this picture held by the average elector of his MP? To what extent are MPs powerless or crooked? In what degree are their powers curtailed and are they indeed, as popular opinion has it, less powerful than they have been in the past?

In order to understand the position of MPs, it is necessary to show a full picture of all the factors affecting them in their representative role. If the public are right to expect MPs to be more effective in representation, more able to control or limit Government, then how can this condition be brought about?

Against the complex background of group pressures, international events, economic crises, social upheaval, industrial trends and rapid technological advance the Member of Parliament is a slender figure. One man against the storm of history. Events have their own logic, they are carried along by cause and effect; by law of inevitability. The MP is in the eyes of the people the man with his finger in the dyke. Jeremy Bray says Parliament imposes 'a whole life context'. There is no area of life and society to which an MP can close his eyes. Yet the overwhelming weight of Parliamentary legislation, the staggering number of responsibilities now extending to every part of the world, make his job almost impossible under present circumstances.

Still the expectations of people in terms of political representation are becoming greater. Democracy is advancing through the spread of education. Participation is becoming an uninvited reality as more and more groups take up cudgels on behalf of causes as wide apart as Rhodesia and the Chunnel. Government is increasingly under pressure from society and increasingly running it. MPs are caught in between. It should be their job to make Government sensitive to public attitudes. Perhaps the very fact that people are taking political opposition more and more into their own hands is a result of the impassivity of Government in the face of Parliamentary opposition. Is there then something wrong with the whole political set up and if so what?

It may be glib to say that Parliament does not work. But this could be true. Certainly it functions after a fashion, but to what end? If Parliament as law maker is finished, or being bent to the wrong ends perhaps the MPs are at fault? If the system is stronger than its participants, there may be something wrong with them. It may be true that MPs are weak, vacillating, hypocritical and dishonest. But it is unlikely that they were all born that way. It is equally unlikely that politicians are indeed 'all the same' as accused, but perhaps there is something in the way of life of Parliament which reduces their zeal, affects their vision, cuts them off from reality. It is all very well to criticise MPs. Most people however only have the vaguest idea of how Parliament should work, of what MPs should be doing.

Moreover, all the factors affecting MPs, the motives, their method of working, the attitudes, their actions need to be understood before that criticism becomes in any way valid.

MPs are a legend. Ideally they should be incorruptible, honourably intentioned, selfless, tireless and virtuous: they should be absolutely faultless in their actions, lucid in analysis, incomparably wise and good. However they are human. Whereas some have a few of these remarkable characteristics, most have a great number of quite normal human weaknesses. If sympathy is in short supply, it may be because MPs live what to some people seems an ideal life. Travel, intrigue, uninhibited extroversion, in general a comfortable life and an exciting lot seems to be theirs. But how true is all this? MPs have to fit in family life between erratic and time consuming political duties. Parliamentary debates alone can keep them up half the night, four nights a week in term time. There are other uncertainties. Money, pensions and other conditions take their toll. Some MPs may seem to be having a wonderful time. But there are many who are never heard of. Who knows how they live? While some MPs appear to be going on foreign delegations, or holidaying in exotic places during political crises, there are others who work as much as ninety hours a week, survive on a breadline and travel thousands of miles in relatively unglamorous circumstances to help their constituents.

The position is endowed in the public eye with a certain glamour. But the rough edges are never seen. Similarly the problems involved in doing Parliamentary work are largely concealed. Subtle factors affect the decisions of MPs. Nothing so open as a bribe or a threat, but tiny pressures operating on the weak spots of human nature move more mountains in MPs minds than any political bulldozer.

The way MPs live, how their families fare, how their private lives suffer or benefit from their Membership of Parliament: the way they are paid, the amount, whether they are happy or not, all affect the way in which Parliament works. Similarly, the power of the Government, the strength of the Whips, the domination of the Party over the individual are all part of the complex influences guiding and controlling MPs. If the nature of Parliament is to be understood, then the politics that lies between the lines of the Parliamentary dialogue must be examined. There is more to Parliament than meets the casual eye. There is more to it than press and media reports can convey. There is more to it than the drive and ambition of individual politicians can explain: more than simply the hard facts of Parliamentary procedures, or the realities of the political system. The essence of our political system is contained in the hearts and minds, the hopes and the consciences of individual politicians and the people who are involved in their lives.

It is that, the thoughts and wishes, the very ordinary human needs and desires, that in the context of Parliament make MPs what they are. That, is what this book is all about. MPs have contributed to it: talked about their lives, their personal and political ambitions, their frustrations, their motives. They have talked on a wider scale about the work of Parliament, the future of democracy and their role as representatives. This is not a survey. It is not a sociological treatise, but more a series of essays which attempt to bring Parliament and its Members down to an ordinary human level.

The political structure, the framework of Government and Parliament are all very well: whether the Constitution is written down or not, it is in the end operated through the foibles of human nature. All politics is about attitudes, about changing people's minds. Parliament is no exception. It has its own politics. Beyond the narrow confines of parties and the small machinations of personal ambition, there are other subtler forces at work. It is these most of all which need to be taken into account in any discussion of reform of Parliament or the electoral system: these are the basis of the politics of Parliament: the forces which turn fairly ordinary idealistic men and women into accomplished politicians. Here, then, is what you should know about your MP.

Part I

THE ROAD
TO WESTMINSTER

I

WHY CHOOSE POLITICS?

In the ideal democracy, political awareness, power and responsibility are equally shared. But if theoretically in Britain, every elector is a potential politician with an equal chance at least of becoming an MP, in practice this is far from true. However, if society is divided, as politicians themselves are fond of saying, into a them and us of politicians and voters it is not so much because barriers to full participation exist — although they do — but because the number of individuals who actually want to become politicians is small.

A surprisingly tiny proportion of the public actually display any interest in politics beyond party allegiance and the vote, and most will preface any political remarks with an apologetic 'of course I don't know anything about politics'. At each General Election between one-fifth and one-quarter of the registered voters fail to vote. At by-elections between 5 and 10 per cent more stay away from the polls and at Local Government elections a meagre third of the voters can be bothered to express their preference. Nationally only some 14 per cent have been found to actually subscribe to a party and as few as 0·03 per cent to hold any party office.*

In proportion to the number of electors the proportion of MPs is likewise small. In February 1974, the electorate of the United Kingdom numbered 39,591,723, and the number of Members serving them increased from 630 to 632 in the boundary reorganisation.

The number of candidates contesting is from two to three times the number of Members, as it is usual for every seat to have two candidates fighting and a varying number to have

* Butler and Stokes, *Political Change in Britain*

three or more. In the watershed election of February 1974, a record 2,165 candidates stood and well over five hundred constituencies had at least three candidates fighting.

So much for an extraordinary enthusiasm for politics shared by parties and voters alike. With more candidates standing and more votes cast than ever before, a greater number of electors voted for defeated candidates and the record number of 1,533 contestants went home after the votes were counted to resume normal life. In later elections some of these may be elected to Parliament. But for most, under the winner takes all electoral system, their contest will have been a gesture; one in which there is no real hope of being elected. Yet it is a gesture that most will enjoy, few will regret and from which some will even profit. Even so, why do they do it?

Profit is seldom the motive of the men and women who stand for Parliament. Contrary to popular belief, politicians start out at least, with pure even if vague intentions. But if profit is not the motive what is?

For every one and a half thousand or so who contest at each General Election there are another two or three thousand waiting in the wings. Party offices, particularly that of the Conservative Party, have no shortage of willing lambs in spite of the fact that few will be allowed to grow to ramhood, and most are for the slaughter. But even including little boys and girls who may have set their hearts on becoming MPs, this number probably never exceeds three thousand: and for each one there are thirty thousand people to whom the thought of entering politics will never occur. What then is different about politicians from the mass of people they may come to represent. What are the motives of these active politicals: and what are the factors which bring them up out of the anonymity of the electorate to demand for themselves a greater say in the workings of the system?

To compare the incipient politician with the seasoned MP is false. His motives are different. Non-politicians are not easy to convince that this is so: electors think politicians 'all the same' and the label sticks like mud. With its inherent insult it brands weak and strong, honest and corrupt, the wayward and the dedicated. With its implied disgust it condemns motives in politicians which in other members of society are accepted without comment. The electorate want honest politicians, yet at the same time they deny that the possibility exists. Selfish motives are not good enough in the people who have been put 'up there' to govern, represent or lead. Purity of motive is required. But is it present?

Purity of political motive produces fanatics as well as men of more acceptable integrity. Hitler, Stalin, Oliver Cromwell and John Birch were all, like Caesar, 'honourable men' in these terms. Selfless devotion and singularity of mind was their hallmark. What they said they meant. Men with a sense of mission or a devotion to changing the world, a belief in their own glorious destiny, and adherence to their cause, all end up in politics. They might not necessarily be right: or they may not, any more than Karl Marx, stand for Parliament. But they are honest in their desire to achieve change and sometimes frightening in their dedication.

The desire to achieve change is not a characteristic of all who enter Parliament. Nor do all radicals choose Parliament as their means of political action. It is fashionable now for young people involved in politics to reject the Parliamentary system as a means of instituting change. Yet, contrary to this there are more young people in Parliament now than ever before; young people who clearly believe that politics leads to Parliament.

In theory a democratic system enables anyone who wants to achieve changes to do so. In our system it is necessary to try quite hard. Outside Parliament there is plenty of publicity for pressure groups, but little power to effect permanent change. Parliament is the home of both executive and legislature. To anyone who has not yet been an MP this offers an opportunity to convert ideal into action, opinion into law. To the more cynical and the realists Parliament offers the opportunity to influence events in unmeasurable tiny ways.

How Parties Can Make MPs

Since to quote Brian Walden, 'the essence of Parliament is

party', those who still believe in power through Parliament gravitate towards the political parties as the first stage in their commitment.

The parties are the most obvious channels of control. They harness opinion, channelling it until it becomes policy. Policy sometimes becomes law; and law is ruler. The theory of power in a democracy is that anyone can influence policy. To anyone looking for more influence the first step is to join a political party, and begin influencing its policy. There is then a logical progression to greater influence within the party.

The step from party membership to MP is shorter than it looks. The party is a vortex. The active and the able are sucked into involvement. Canvassing, committees, offices come the way of the promising young people. A council election, chairmanship of the youth organisation, a speech here and there, will soon lead to the first offers of a Parliamentary constituency. Wil Edwards, previously Labour Member for Merioneth says, 'Particularly in rural areas you get rapidly promoted. Talent is in short supply.' A great number of MPs have come to the House by this process. Politicians are considered especially ambitious creatures. If they are, it is not necessarily for themselves. There are certainly rich rewards in politics for the man who deliberately seeks them; but the ambition of most politicians to start with are mainly ambition for their ideas. It is this quality most of all which make politicians seem dangerous to non-political people; which makes them so hard to understand.

The hierarchical system of parties gives the politician the incentive to apply for Parliamentary candidature as the highest possible means of achieving success for his ideas. There may be other ways: to be leader of the IRA; a Trade Union boss; the editor of an underground magazine, or even Mrs. Mary Whitehouse, is a means of achieving some political power and change. But so often the people who achieve positions of political influence outside Parliament become absorbed into it. They become Members of Parliament and so often are never really heard of again. The system absorbs its dissidents by rewarding them with Parliamentary office. Parliament however has for them the advantage that it gives weight to political opinions which would otherwise fall fruitlessly between the lines of newspaper articles. It gives position and prestige. Even a fool, and there are some in Parliament, may be thought respectable.

Ambitions of High Office

The stage by stage progress of an individual towards candidature is virtually one of conversion to the idea of the importance of Parliament as a means to achieving a political end. Commitment to party is like initiation into drug taking. At each stage, the political individual will spot a better opportunity to exert his influence. New goals develop along the way.

John Gorst says: 'I was attracted into politics while working for Pye.' His company encouraged his political interest which later became an obsession with private enterprise. When he first attempted to become a Conservative candidate he was refused for not being in the party long enough; but having decided to become a candidate, Gorst changed his whole way of life and work, subordinating them to his campaign to get into Parliament. In 1970 he was elected. 'It took me,' he says, with almost a groan, 'ten years.' Now he would like Ministerial office but says: 'You can only look to the next immediate stage.' Brian Walden agrees with him. There is a tendency to hedge bets. 'The whole things,' says Gorst, 'is out of ones own control.'

There is some evidence that men go into Parliament with their eyes on office. The prospect of becoming Prime Minister may lurk in the minds of the deeply ambitious. Marcus Lipton is one who admits that he did want high office. 'I wanted,' he says, 'to be a big shot, to be Prime Minister. I wanted to sway people, lead them. I always wanted to be a politician.' This is in contrast to Brian Walden who says that he stood for Parliament to please his friend Hugh Gaitskell, liked the experience and fought again. Whereas Marcus Lipton says: 'I quickly realised my limitations,' however, Walden is proud of reaching the front benches. Horizons change once a man is elected. But the initial drive to get into Parliament is based on a variety of motives for most.

The Personal and Personality Factors

Such is the complex motivation of politicians that personal rather than political reasons can bring a man into politics. 'Do not underestimate,' says Brian Walden, 'the power of a man's private life. There are,' he says, 'men in Parliament who have gone into politics to get away from their wives.' Politics is certainly the ideal substitute for a destitute private life. There are emotional cripples in all the social and economic groups and their reactions to their conditions are never contemplative. Hard work, constant occupation and movement are great distractions from the problems of the inner man. I have certainly met Members of Parliament who come into this category. On the surface they may be perfectly normal; aggressive, egotistical, flamboyant, obsessive perhaps, but in this not distinguishable from people in other jobs. With one exception. They have the perfect alibi for almost never going home to their families or for that matter to themselves. They are shielded from being real people by the posture of being public men. They become, in the words of ex-Member and Minister Dr. Jeremy Bray, 'complete victims of their own public image'.

There is nothing so Freudian however in the motivations of those who clearly see, not merely the way to pass the time, or be the centre of attention, or even to see their dreams of a new civilisation wrought by their own hands, but an excellent business opportunity. To the young grey suited executive of the seventies, getting to Parliament is as good a leg up in the business world as 'coming out' is to a young girl in society. New opportunities occur to make and use influential connections: to use special knowledge for directorships and consultancies, to gain advance information for advantageous business deals and investments, even on a rather lesser scale to become a star of the TV screen. Such chances do come less easily to the unelected. How many prospective candidates are influenced by these opportunities would be impossible to guess. That they should be motivated by this alone is unlikely except for the rarest cases. I know at least one such Member, but one is not a trend.

Jeremy Bray describes Parliament as 'a cockpit of human personality. A place where the extremes are exaggerated, the saints more saintly, the sinners more sinful.' Politicians are on the whole more extrovert characters; but once in Parliament personality can run riot. Politicians are not expected to be mousy. Perhaps this fact too attracts men to stand for Parliament. Theatrical abilities are often the cause of theatrical behaviour: and what in its more contentious aspects could offer more opportunity for such talents than Parliament?

These are lesser motives. They contribute to the whole compulsion towards politics. Showmanship, the desire to interfere, to lead, to be Prime Minister; the love of rhetoric, of the limelight, even of the human race can all contribute to the total bundle of political motivation. The fact that a man comes from a political family, like the Asquiths, the Lloyd Georges, the Churchills, may influence his ambitions towards politics. Perhaps even an ambition planted by a doting relative during one of those 'and what are you going to be when you grow up' sessions can work in the unconscious mind of the politician: as in the case of ex-Member Miss Janet Fookes, who says: 'I don't know why. I always wanted to be an MP — even as a little girl.'

For Queen, Country or Class

At one time Parliament was a respectable occupation-cum-club for the stupidest sons of squirarchy. It was the last resort of men who could do nothing else. Times have changed.

With enfranchisement of the workers, class politics became a Parliamentary issue. The growth of the Trade Union movement culminating in the foundation of the Labour Party in 1900 created a new breed of Parliamentary candidates. Men with a real class motive, unlike the Liberals who had not been

23

battling for their own class but for the broad principles of humanity, now stood for Parliament. The Labour Party now matched self-interest with self-interest and the class struggle reached Parliamentary politics.

The prime political call had always been to duty: to what Lloyd George called 'great and honourable public service'. Class interest brought into the open changed all that. Hard lines which we now recognise as party politics began to form. There is still a difference between motivation of Members on the two sides of the House: an element of Gentlemen *v.* Players. Conservatives appear to be much less 'political' than Labour and Liberal Members. They talk less of change and reform. They were called to politics not to change the world, or even to keep it as it is, but to organise and serve. John Gorst is one of the few Conservatives who has genuine political motivation. He is in effect a right wing radical.

For Labour, the reverse is true. Labour candidates are motivated to put Labour Party policy into the Statute Book. They may, as Jeremy Thorpe once accused, 'stand on their heads' when they get into Parliament; but initially, they serve the Labour cause, at least verbally.

Basic political motivation or a sense of civic duty may be enough to bring a man into a political party: factors such as ambition, extroversion, opportunism and talent may push him towards candidature; but there are other qualities and conditions to be taken into account.

From Gentlemen to Some Kinds of Players

Gentlemen of private means on both sides of the House have given way gradually to those earning their own money. The next best thing to a private fortune is income from private interests: for instance from a profession. The fact that the House is, apart from its Trade Union sponsored Members and a high proportion of teachers, almost entirely populated by professional or self-employed men suggests a correlation between the means of employment and the inclination to stand for Parliament.

24

Parliament is dominated by a few professional groups. Lawyers, for instance, represent one-sixth of the total number of MPs: fifty-six Conservative and thirty-four Labour barristers, and eleven Conservative and twelve Labour solicitors add up to a total of one hundred and sixteen lawyers. In February 1974 there was one less elected. Journalists are another well represented group. Teachers and lecturers, on the increase, are now the second biggest category. In 1955 there were forty-three, in 1970 sixty-five, and now seventy-six — of whom sixty-nine are Labour.

What is it that attracts so many of these few professional types to Parliament? One interesting feature of teachers, journalists and lawyers is that they are all what is termed communicators. Add to this the fact that there is a growing representation of public relations men, and it would seem that Parliament attracts talkers and writers.

Lawyers have an added interest in Parliament. It is logical that anyone who works with the law sees its deficiencies. It is natural that the purveyors of law would want to be associated with reforming and streamlining the whole machine. There is much in common between the life of law and the life of politics: and there is little difference between standing up in court to defend a client and standing up in Parliament to attack the Government.

Another quality of Parliamentary representatives is that with the exception of the Trade Union contingent of miners, engineers, carpenters and railwaymen, Parliament is overwhelmingly middle class, self-employed and professional in its representation. With the exception of the forty-six managers, some of whom would have come from industry, the remainder is made up of stockbrokers (20); the landowners and farmers (33); company directors (87); the accountants (12); the journalists (56); the PR men, publishers (2); and (4) respectively, also medicals (10).* Two-thirds of the House is accounted for by self-employed professional men.

* All figures for successive Parliaments to be found in *Times Guide to the House of Commons* and Macmillan's series, *The British General Election* by Butler and King.

The advantage of self-employment is greatest during candidature. Self-employment makes it easier for a man to take time off work and to fit his campaigning in with his occupation. After election lawyers and journalists, TV people and public relations men are particularly able to carry on, part-time at least with their former occupations while doing the work of MPs. This also applies to stockbrokers, gentlemen farmers, company directors, but not so much to managers and medicals.

The fact that there are no butchers, bakers, candlestick makers, window cleaners, charladies, hairdressers, strippers, models, bookies, dress designers, painters or news vendors in the House may suggest that there are other factors at work. Certainly these jobs are less easily carried on after election: but then perhaps political people choose jobs with the same elements as political life.

The Shift in Age Group Patterns

If the middle classes dominate the House of Commons, so do the middle aged. To less fashionable groups in society this can hardly be imagined. Of course there are aristocrats and working class men in the House, likewise, septuagenarians (five) and people in their twenties. The trend towards younger Members is however increasing, although it is the 40 to 60 age groups who dominate. In the 1970 General Election, 412 Members — more than two-thirds of the entire House were between these ages. In actual fact the spread of ages describes a beautiful statistical curve — a sort of bell shape. However, the curve is changing shape, and there is an increased trend towards youth.

The highest number of MPs for any age group in 1970 was 213 (as against 186 in 1966) in the 40 to 50 age group: in 1974 this rose to 238. The middle age spread in the statisticians bulge has dropped a whole notch from above to below the 50 year belt.

Further enhancement of the trend to youth took place in February 1974. Whereas in 1955 there were 425 Members between the ages of 40 and 60, there were still more (135) over

60 than under 40. The 1970–74 Parliament contained roughly equal numbers of over-60s and under-40s. But in February 1974, with only 338 Members between 40 and 60, the bulk of the remainder (130) was under 40 as compared to only 83 over 60 — a virtual reversal of the 1955 situation. More Tory Members than Labour were under 55.

Unsuccessful candidates as a whole tend to have a younger average age than MPs. In 1959 for instance when the highest number of successful candidates fell into the 50–60 age group, the highest number of unsuccessful ones fell between 30 and 40.*

The underlying causes of these trends may well lie with the selection committees and the electors rather than with the deep seated motivations of potential candidates. It may be the greater trend towards career politics which attracts potential candidates at a younger age, in larger numbers; and similarly deters the over-40s from standing if they have not done so before. There are notable exceptions to this rule. One is John Davies, Secretary of State for Trade and Industry, who was lured from his high position in Shell to stand for a safe seat in the 1970 General Election; his first try at the hustings.

The Special Mould

If candidates are becoming younger, they are also becoming more uniform. Trends are towards admass men, Grammar School educations and Red Brick graduates as against Public School, Oxbridge, on the one hand and elementary school and the pithead on the other.

Marcus Lipton remarked to me in disgust, 'I can't tell the difference between some of these young Tory Members sitting across the chamber from me.' He went on: 'They look the same and they sound the same, and if you close your eyes you can't tell which one is speaking. I think there must be a factory somewhere churning them out.'

Perhaps this is what the electors mean when they accuse politicians of being 'all the same'. Whatever motives politicians

* *British General Election 1959* — Butler and King.

start out with, their behaviour tends to look the same. There is a pattern of political behaviour to which all politicians come to conform. The system of selection, the requirements of selection committees, the narrow corridors of possible action, all help to push politicians into a particular mould. But if they look alike and behave alike, if they come from a similar background or a particular age group, they do not necessarily think alike. Politicians, MPs particularly may be unrepresentative of the population in terms of class and professional background, but in terms of political opinion they are widely divergent and completely representative.

In this one aspect they do not differ from non-political people: they share their opinions. Motivation apart, MPs are fairly human. The progress of the political individual from first political act to becoming a seasoned MP is one of slow sophistication.

In that process lie all the pitfalls which change possibly honest men into the contemporary image of the political figure. Political sophistication is essential. It does not go hand in hand with length of service. It can come quickly to some and never to others. The dangers of this gradual seasoning are that it removes the good qualities with the bad. One man I spoke to said a Minister friend had become 'less human' over the years of their acquaintance. Looking at many senior politicians it is possible to see that they lack the most important quality of all — compassion. Motives apart, we are all lost if our rulers lack that one.

2

WHO CHOOSES MPs?

If motivation, inclination and opportunity are vital factors in deciding who wants to become an MP, selection is even more crucial: the process actually decides the nature of the House of Commons. Two-thirds of the seats in the country are safe seats, i.e. with between 17 and 31 per cent majorities or impregnable seats, i.e. with over 31 per cent majorities. In these seats the constituency party is entirely responsible for the choice of the MP. Thus in two-thirds of constituencies the MP is chosen by sometimes less than a majority of one hundred people.

For instance a seat like Chichester, which had a majority of 42 per cent for the Conservatives in 1970, or Ebbw Vale where Michael Foot had a 70·3 per cent majority in 1966 are entirely in the hands of the executive of the winning party. Nothing short of a boundary change is likely to break the hold of the entrenched. Anyone who gets selected for a seat of this sort is bound to be elected: moreover he has the seat for life barring accidents or 'bad' behaviour.

The only exceptions to this rule occur occasionally in by-elections where a safe seat for one party owes much of its majority to the personality of the deceased Member. If the by-election occurs during a period of disaffection for the entrenched party, the seat can be taken by a candidate for another party. Often Liberals and Nationalists win by-elections in this type of seat and frequently lose them back to the original holders in a General Election.

Only in one-third of the country is there any uncertainty on the part of the selectors that their choice will win a majority: only in one-sixth is there any susceptibility to a swing of less than 6 per cent. Anyone with a majority of more than 10 per cent is in a fairly good position for most elections. Selection then mostly means certain election for candidates of the entrenched party.

The Traditional Pattern

Candidates usually fight one or two unwinnable seats before being offered a good one. This is the standard pattern in all parties. There are exceptions. First-timers do get offered winnable seats. Jonathan Aitken for instance was adopted for Malton and Thirsk* without having cut his teeth on anything other than a sandwich. Usually this depends upon pull with the party leadership. Aitken is after all Beaverbrook's grandson. Similarly Gerald Kauffman, a faithful Wilson aid, was rewarded with the semi-marginal seat of Manchester Ardwick to which he was elected in 1970.

Most candidates go through the prover according to the habit of the party concerned. Selection procedures vary considerably between parties. There is a basic pattern which is the same in all. That is, the central party takes an interest and the constituency party has the final say. The differences relate to the variation in emphasis placed on central party 'advice' and local autonomy. The prize for the most democratic method of selection goes easily to the Labour Party. Here, at least in most cases, an attempt is made to see that each stage is fair and subject to the decision of representatives of the various groups involved.

The Conservative Party has its own rather unique style best known for the interest expressed by selectors in the candidates' wives. The smaller parties tend to be less democratic in their selection procedures: perhaps because they experience more difficulty in recruiting candidates in the first place, because the choice open to selection committees if therefore smaller, and because the selection committees themselves are drawn from smaller groups than the two major parties.

* Aitken later had to withdraw as candidate owing to his prosecution under the Official Secrets Act over an article published in the *Daily Telegraph* during the later stages of the Nigerian civil war.

The Liberals used to have difficulty maintaining the quality of candidates, and even any adoption rate at all after the 200 mark. This is largely because of the essential difficulties of getting candidates elected from a third party position in a dominantly two-party system. Asking a Liberal to get elected is like expecting the referee to score a goal. Consequently there is less of a rush for candidature. But any upswing in Liberal fortunes tends to be followed by an onrush of potential candidates. Following the series of by-election successes scored by Liberals in 1972 and 1973, Liberals were riding high in the opinion polls and the Liberal Party Candidates' Department was receiving nine applications a day in the latter part of 1973. As a result the party fielded 517 candidates in February 1974 and for the first time in fifty years became a credible alternative at the polls.

But the ability of Liberal candidates to get elected under the winner-takes-all-system is still severely limited. Trebling their vote in the country Liberals still ended up with only fourteen — an increase of two — MPs. The influence of Liberal selection committees on the contents of the House of Commons must still therefore be considered small.

As far as Labour and Tory selection committees are concerned, the reverse is true, and the Liberal impact makes their position the more extraordinary. In 1970, 28,344,807 people voted (72 per cent poll). The 13,144,692 (46·4 per cent) Conservative voters were represented by 330 MPs, and the 12,179,166 (42·9 per cent) Labour voters by 287 Members. In 1974 the impact of Liberals and others proportionately increased the power of the Tory and Labour selection committees in relation to the number of votes cast. The 298 Conservative MPs were elected with a nationwide support of 11,928,677 votes (38·1 per cent) and the 301 Labour Members with 11,661,488 (37·2 per cent). Meanwhile the 6,056,713 Liberal voters influenced the contents of the House to the tune of fourteen Members.

The results for Nationalist candidates, who had one Member elected for roughly every hundred thousand votes cast were rather more proportionate. Nevertheless the safe seats are mostly still in the hands of the Conservative and Labour Party selectors. Most of the Tory and Labour Members have majorities over 6 per cent and most were probably selected by constituency selection committees of less than one hundred. In some constituencies this could be from a choice of six or seven candidates and in others from as few as two or three, one of whom could easily be a weighted candidate from party HQ.

The level of interference from the central administration of the parties varies according to factors such as whether the contest is an important by-election, whether there is a need to elect someone who is to be a Minister — for instance John Davies in 1970. Better still a Prime Minister; witness the election/selection of Alec Douglas Home, then Lord Home, Fourteenth Earl on his ascension to the leadership of the Conservative Party in 1962.

The Conservatives now have a more democratic method of electing their leaders. The habit of prompting candidature however remains, as it does in all parties. Labour were no less guilty, during their period of office between 1964 and 1970. Several candidates were recommended by Transport House to constituency parties with an 'or else' label attached, starting with the unfortunate Patrick Gordon Walker — a rare example of a party plant that failed to get a rubber stamp of approval from the electorate. He had to be foisted on to Leyton for the by-election there after failing to get in at Smethwick in the 1964 General Election, but lost the by-election and was not elected until the 1966 General Election, a fact that spoilt Harold Wilson's plan to make him Foreign Secretary.

There are times when the local party refuses to accept a strong recommendation from the central organisation. Reg Underhill, Head of the Labour Party candidates department, speaks for all parties when he said 'local parties do not like to be dictated to'. There are occasions too when the electorate shows that it will not be dictated to by a local party. Former MPs who stand as independents in their own constituencies when they have lost the support of their local party are frequently elected. Unfortunately these occasions are all too rare and the local party selection committee or the powers that be nationally are the people who decide the name and nature of most MPs.

The Labour Party Selection Process

The autonomy of the local Labour Party in the selection process is unmatched by other parties. The only adherance to any central influence is in the rules followed. In a neat little book small enough to be kept next to the heart, entitled, *Constitution and Rules for Constituency Labour Parties in Divided and Undivided Boroughs*, the party sets out the regulations for candidate selection. The rules show a certain reverence for the hygiene of democracy.

The Labour Party, youngest of any of the parties to have held office in Britain, is perhaps most fascinating because of its federal origins. It is these origins which, even now, seventy odd years after the foundation of the Labour Party, provide the nominations within the local party for Parliamentary candidature: and also the delegates to the selection conference.

Each body is entitled to one nomination. This then goes forward to the various vetting processes that are essential before the nominations are validated. The National Executive has to approve the nominations and then the process of selection is set in motion: again this is according to rules specifically set down by the National Executive. Reg Underhill insists that the part played by Transport House in all this is purely administrative. The delicate machine of intra-party democracy is only supervised from the centre.

There are occasional exceptions. At by-elections, for instance, the normal rules are superseded. The National Executive or presumably any other Tom, Dick or Harold who happens to have a good enough reason for putting a nomination forward can have the whole machine behind his individual choice. This says Underhill is necessary 'because by-election candidates need to be of a high standard'.

Normally, what happens is that a selection conference is convened, consisting of a specific number of delegates from the

33

various affiliated groups of the local party. All details of the convening, assembling and voting of the delegates is strictly controlled. For instance no delegate who has not heard all of the speakers at a selection conference or the whole speech of all of the nominees is allowed to vote on the selection.

When the speakers have been heard — each for a fixed and equal time and questioned to the satisfaction of the audience, voting takes place until only one candidate remains! This being the finalist in the stakes for prospective Parliamentary candidate. All that remains now is for final approval to come from the National Executive Committee.

Most times, this approval is forthcoming but Underhill cites an occasion during the period of the last Labour Government's greatest unpopularity with its supporters when a candidate was refused approval. The grounds, not entirely inexplicable to students of Transport House or any other organisation with powers of censorship, were that the candidate with the support of the local party wished to fight a by-election on an anti-Government platform.

Quite naturally, Transport House refused to validate the candidature. There was no reason why the local party should not have gone ahead and fought on its anti-Government ticket. It would undoubtedly have received considerable electoral support. But probably there were valid reasons of finance and co-operation why it did not.

Sticking to party policy by the letter is a vital part of the acceptability of candidates to the Labour Party. Strikingly, in a party which sets such store by democratic method, there is a remarkable devotion to toeing-the-party-line. The Conservatives rarely pillory their deviants with the fanaticism of the Labour Party. A gentleman's conscience is presumably his own, and his loyalty to monarch and country indisputable. Should a Conservative decide to speak out against his party, his leader or their policies, he is unlikely to be disciplined.

In the Labour Party, however, the candidate is expected to platform the views of the party in preference to his own. This does not mean to say that he is not permitted any of his own. It is simply that the cracks of the federal composition of the

Labour Party show through the wallpaper rather more readily than in other parties.

There are permissible deviations. Some controversies, no longer topical will not bias selection. Views contrary to party policy may be acceptable to the party at one time though not at another. For instance, it is doubtful whether the views of a Labour candidate on CND would cause much of a stir these days whatever they happened to be; but in the late fifties they would have been crucial. Between 1966 and 1974 the Common Market was the issue of decision.

Advice to policy deviants would appear to be to play a straight bat on topical battles and show any independence required on out of season topics.

About half of the present Parliamentary Labour Party is made up of Trade Union and Co-op nominations. The nature of the Parliamentary Labour Party has been changing in recent years with altogether younger and more middle class candidates being selected. The selection committees have clearly been opting for a different type of candidate. Underhill explains this readily as being due to the shift in the balance of groups to be represented. He also insists on the devoutly representative nature of selection conferences choices. He points out that the number of National Union of Miners sponsored MPs has been falling gradually in recent years. In 1959 thirty-six miners stood as candidates. Thirty-four of these were elected. In 1970 only twenty miners entered Parliament from a group of twenty-one candidates. Underhill explains this as being a natural decline related to the decline in the mining communities which until the oil crisis of 1973 had been steadily in progress throughout the sixties. Thirty-seven miners of whom four — amazingly enough — were Conservatives entered Parliament in 1955. And in spite of the miners' strike being an important factor in February 1974, only sixteen miners' union candidates were elected to Parliament.

Underhill further illustrates his argument with the example of the engineering unions. Engineering is an increasingly important industry. In 1955 engineers were not even represented as a parliamentary category, yet in the 1970–74 Parliament there

35

were twenty-two engineer members. This further increased to twenty-seven in 1974.

If marketing men are now as predominant in the Labour Party as union men this is not something which comes across. The public can be forgiven for thinking that the Trades Union tail wags the Labour Party dog when the voting figures at conferences — several million for or against a motion — give a false impression of the numerical power of that section of the party. The fact is that every Trade Union member, whether he supports the Labour Party or not, is still counted as one of its members. Likewise a portion of his subscription is contributed to the party as a levy. Then, again, Trade Union money flows into the Labour Party coffers at election time. On the other hand the Labour Party arose from the Trade Union movement and has always been a federation of Trades Unionists and socialists, the latter on the whole very much in the minority until recently. Trades Union sponsored MPs are now a smaller proportion of the Parliamentary Labour Party than in the past.

Trade Union candidates are selected much on the same pattern as any other Labour Party candidates. Like non-union candidates their names appear initially on a central list held by the candidates department at Transport House. These lists, known simply as List A (Trade Union nominations) and List B (other nominations), are circulated to all constituency parties. Unlike the list in the Conservative Party, and that in the Liberal Party, the candidates have not been thoroughly vetted by the central organisation. They are simply on the list because they have been nominated either by a body within a constituency party or by a Trade Union. Central vetting in the Labour Party comes after selection. The selected candidate may have been nominated locally. 'Central interference would,' says Reg Underhill, 'not be tolerated under any circumstances, until afterwards. My advice may be sought, but only off the record.'

In the Conservative and Liberal Parties, the lists compiled by the central organisations are the most important source of candidates. These lists differ from the Transport House and Trade Union lists in that they are built up from individuals who have already been interviewed and approved. Whereas the Labour Party lists are of nominations for selection and approval, the Liberal and Tory party lists are already approved.

How the Conservatives Choose

In the case of the Conservative Party the initial interviewing is carried out by the Vice-Chairman of the Party who is usually a Member of Parliament: and further by a central selection committee before the chosen candidates' names go on the list.

Clearly much depends on the personality of the initial interviewer and the opinions of this person as to what kind of individual makes a good candidate: and perhaps more interestingly a good Member of Parliament.

The Vice-Chairman of the Conservative Party has an onerous task. Mr. William Elliott has held this office since June 1970. (His predecessor was the late Sir Richard Sharples.) It is unlikely that personal preferences result in the rejection of talented individuals. But the taste of the vetter could influence the order of preference in a recommendation to constituency parties.

His recommendations may reflect the preferences of the Party leader for one type of education or another type of political attitude. Bill Elliott says: 'One must always try to be fair,' and there is no doubt that he is sincere. He recognises the difficulties one man has in making a judgment of any other. But there is nothing to suggest that a group of individuals would come to a better decision.

Even a computer programmed for all the desirable qualities of candidates would not necessarily select the right individuals. There are a few major qualities which must be there. Elliott says: 'I look for the light in their eyes.' This romantic sounding phrase is an expression of the intuitive method that one individual uses to judge another: that subconscious computing process by which a man decides on the nature and desires of another. He looks for 'a sense of duty, a desire to serve ones country and its people'. Good paternalistic stuff, but a politician that lacks these qualities may turn out to be amoral and a charlatan.

Patriotism has always been an essential part of the Conservative public image. Meeting platforms draped with the Union Jack, the singing of Land of Hope and Glory are a part of Conservative ritual. In contrast the Red Flag with its more international 'workers of the world' appeal is regarded by Tories as the shameful badge of subversion and treachery. Such are the trappings of party politics.

Love of country is the basis of the sense of duty that Bill Elliott looks for in his candidates. In addition he says: 'One has to feel, to be sensitive, one must be proud to be an MP.' He is on the right track. The converse of these qualities are callousness, self-interest, a lack of respect for humanity: qualities so often found among hardened criminals. Politicians become subject to many temptations. It is well that they should be screened for ethics and humanity before they start.

Humour is another quality which Elliott feels essential. So many politicians are vain and pompous. 'They would not be,' says Elliott, 'if they could only laugh at themselves.' For all the paternalism of the Conservative selection machine, there is a great deal to be said for one man vetting when the man is Mr. Elliott. After talking to him one is left with the feeling that if he could choose the entire House of Commons Membership we would all be happier people.

Personal choice is not as free as all that, even for the Conservative Vice-Chairman. Elliott says that it is not only a matter of choosing people with the right basic qualities, but 'you have to bear in mind what a constituency selection committee will find acceptable'. In the Labour Party, Reg Underhill is not obliged to involve himself in this. However, constituency parties often ask him for a suitable recommendation. He then may mention one or two names that he thinks would be suitable for the constituency.

The requirements of selection committees change over a period of time. There are certainly fashions among selection committees. The wave of right wing by-election candidates standing for Conservative seats during the late sixties was a result of a right wing bachlash in the constituencies. One such local party backlash nearly dislodged Niger Fisher in mid-term: and at times the wave looked threatening enough to remove Edward Heath from the leadership of the Party. The Conservative win in the 1970 General Election took the pressure off Heath for a time. As a result, more moderate Heath-style candidates were once more selected.

Candidates come for interviews with Bill Elliott from various sources. Many come from the twelve key organisers in the regions. These get to hear of potential candidates who are then referred to the Vice-Chairman. The organisers make their own assessments of suitability. Sometimes they mention that someone should be given an interview for the sake of face in spite of the fact that they lack the essential qualities. Most candidates will, however, be given an interview in good faith.

The Conservative Party Vice-Chairman then makes his own recommendations on the basis of his personal judgment. The answers given by candidates on the central office form are important; so are the comments made by sponsors on another set of forms. Two or preferably three sponsors are required, one of whom, should if possible be an MP. The forms are extensive and include questions as to whether the candidate has done any public speaking, or any public service. Sponsors are asked whether they know of any incident or characteristic of the candidate which might cause embarrassment to him or his constituency party.

Service to the party is important. Very new party members may be asked, as John Gorst was, to re-apply in a year. The same applies in the Labour and Liberal Parties. The most important question asked of Labour candidates is whether they agree to support the adopted policy of the party at all times. Promises are easily given and again very new party members are not encouraged to stand.

In the Conservative Party, the name of the nominating candidate is then submitted to the Standing Advisory Committee which vets them again, though this time only from their papers.

The candidates department of the Liberal Party consists of a curiously vestigial organisation known as the Liberal Central Association. The candidates officer is the Secretary of the Association. He, like Bill Elliott, gives the candidate his first interview. Later the candidate will be called to an interview with the Candidates Selection Committee. Inevitably in the past this used to consist of an odd rabble of Parliamentary candidates — usually of very long standing. The present method of selection was laid down by a consultant specialising in interviewing techniques. The old method of arbitrary judgment after a rather haphazard conversational half-hour with one or two members of the panel has now been streamlined. Candidates are still interviewed by a panel made up often of existing candidates: but this time they are looking for definite qualities.

The candidates are interviewed, preferably separately, by each member of the panel. This prevents one panel member from hogging time and also from directing the questioning along his own pet lines. Further guidance has been given to Liberal interviewers as to the qualities they should look for and the standard they should require. Each interviewer is given a form on which he is able to mark grades A to E for four basic capacities — intellectual ability, motivation, ability to adapt and skill dealing with people. Listed candidates become available for selection by constituencies, and in 1974 most constituency parties were using proportional representation and full meetings of the local Association in the selection process.

The Liberal Party does not insist that constituencies adopt listed candidates. Most Liberal candidates are selected by the officer of the local party ringing the candidate of their choice and asking him to go down for an interview. Central party approval is a rubber stamp in these cases rather like the Transport House checking procedure, but less of a controlling device. Liberal Associations having selected their candidate would not necessarily bother whether the candidate got Head Office approval or not. On the other hand the Party Leadership has on occasion tried to prevent the adoption of a certain candidate for a certain seat and succeeded. But this sort of thing happens in the other parties too. The straightforward procedures are often fraught with manoeuvres and machinations between factions. Personal political enmity between a leading party Member is sometimes the cause of a candidate being dropped at the adoption altar. There have been cases in all parties of adoption meetings voting against the Executive nominee after a rogue ballot.

Malpractices, Abbreviations and Problems in Selection

Reg Underhill says the selection conference in which Michael O'Halloran was first chosen as candidate for Islington North came under scrutiny because 'an awful lot of new members came from somewhere rather suddenly'. In 1968 the Liberals had trouble in a constituency where they wished to select a new candidate. The previous candidate did not want to stand down. A young Liberal received the nomination of the Executive and an adoption meeting was arranged as a formality. On the evening, however, a coach load of supporters arrived waving party membership cards (rather recently acquired) and voted against the nominee.

In the Conservative Party, the control that Central Office maintains over the formal selection procedure eliminates this kind of malpractice. Strange things can still happen but only to Central Office approved candidates.

Once on the Central Office list, the candidate will then be recommended to constituencies as and when the opportunities arise. Some will be unlucky and remain on the list indefinitely; not even asked to go to interview for a seat. Ability helps a candidate get selected, but so also do wealth, personality and charm. Without any obvious outstanding qualities a candidate is stuck on the list where he can remain for as long as twenty years.

When a party is in office with all the safe and winnable seats filled by relatively young men, the other candidates on the list are forced to compete fiercely for the few remaining seats.

Older Members have in the past remained as the title holders of seats long after their usefulness to the constituency has been reduced. The only hope for a listed candidate under these circumstances is for a few of the old leaves to wilt.

Timing is all in politics. A candidate can fight an election in his mid-twenties and be in the House first go, like Peter Kirk. On the other hand, Andrew Bowden fought his first election in 1955 and was not elected until 1970. Bowden made it in the nick of time. To have lost one more election would have made him too old to win the favours of the selection committee: but his experience is a common one. Elections usually happen once every four or five years. One cannot hope for more than three in a decade under normal circumstances. That leaves by-elections. For most candidates a bad choice of seat or bad luck with the political tide can put them out of the running after two fights. A first fight at 35 is often the last. Selection committees are not looking for men much over 40.

The trend against older candidates is also beginning to affect MPs. The Conservative Party, anxious to make way for the queue of younger contenders dabbled with dynamite in the form of the recommendations of the Chelmer Committee. The Committee outlined new rules for the selection and adoption of candidates which included the following bombshell: 'A Member wishing to continue at Westminster must submit himself for re-adoption.' The constituency association concerned, the recommendation goes on 'should have the right to consider other candidates should they so wish'.

This right has always been the unspoken one. Now the Conservatives, of all parties, have put it into print. Constituency associations in all parties have always dropped candidates when they chose to do so. Unless there is any dissatisfaction, the tendency is to keep on with the same old Member. The prospect of new blood in competition with the old at every General Election might, however, help to keep Members on their toes where constituency parties are concerned.

Ben Whittaker is an ex-Labour MP who says that it is a fundamental democratic principle that there should be a fresh choice at every election. He says, 'I tried to get Hampstead

Labour Party to consider choosing someone else, because I think it is right that they should have the opportunity of doing so.'

This unusually noble behaviour is only possible because Ben Whittaker was not certain that he wanted to go to Parliament again. Most ex-MPs join the queue for the next available seat — witness the undignified scramble for safe seats after the boundary reorganisation which took effect in 1974 — and most MPs hang on to their position until sacked by constituents, local party or Father Time. Likewise most unsuccessful candidates stay on the party lists. Hope springs eternal. Like the lady who fails to notice she needs a face-lift, these ageing starlets drift on through the lists, waiting for the call that never comes.

These can become a problem. Lists become unwieldy, and where it would be kinder to leave men in their sixties and seventies listed, it becomes impossible to do so. After 1970 the Conservative Party pared its list down by asking more than 500 candidates to withdraw their names. At the time, William Elliott, who had received instructions from Mr. Heath, came in for a great deal of abuse — from the *Daily Telegraph* and from the candidates themselves. Inhumane though his act may have seemed, Elliott bowed to protest and invited anyone who did not feel happy about being asked to resign from the list to come and see him. To his horror, over 400 accepted the invitation: throughout the spring of 1971 he sat in his office and listened to their complaints.

Resign they all did in the end. Polite invitations for interviews were after all only a prolongation of the sack.

Ex-MPs were among the number, almost all of whom were simply too old, in the views of the administration, to stand again. It is worth asking whether these unlucky 500 might not have included a number of old-style Tories. The probability of that is high. Mr. Heath would hardly be looking for more of the kind of Tory with whom he had had so much trouble. The excision of 500 names from the list would certainly make room for a few more Heath men to queue for selection. And queue they do.

New potential candidates are being interviewed every week. On most interview days, and there are about three every week, Elliott talks to anything up to a dozen new people. He has currently about two thousand names on his list. One has a right to wonder what, if anything, will make some of those candidates more attractive than others to the constituency selection committees. The powers of the Vice-Chairman are only to recommend. He himself may pass candidates for the list together with the Advisory Committee, but when individual constituencies begin to look for a candidate he can but send them suitable individuals from the list with appropriate recommendations.

The Desirable Candidate

Fashions may change, but there is no denying the predominance of the Tory ladies in selection committees. Their preferences more than any others influence the nature of the candidates put up by the party — indeed those who get onto William Elliott's list. Certain kinds of individual are less likely to be popular than others. 'Women, for instance,' says Bill Elliott, 'are the least desirable brand of candidate' among Tory ladies. Neither are they popular in the Labour Party. The Liberal Party finds them more acceptable; as it also approves of and adopts coloured immigrants as candidates. Liberalism is fashionable at times in the Liberal Party. Likewise, Conservatism wins hands down at almost every Tory selection meeting.

There is a pattern emerging among candidates in all parties at the moment which is somewhat disturbing and more than a little monotonous. If the ideal candidate of any party should be described by any selection committee he would undoubtedly be a man in his middle thirties; married with a nice wife and a couple of children; on his way up in some respectable middle class profession. For good measure he should be white, preferably non-Jewish, and reasonably good to look at.

There is no spoken prejudice against bachelors, women, foreigners or even the unbeautiful; but the underlying feeling in both the major parties is that the electorate might not care for them and therefore they could lose votes from the regular band of supporters.

Talking to the men at the party headquarters, it becomes more easily apparent that elections are usually won on the abstentions of the other side rather than on any vast positive transfer of votes from one side to the other. Votes do change sides, and there are copious figures available to show how, where and when they do. Usually it is the electors' response to national political events rather than the nature of the individual candidate which counts. A candidate considered offensive or unsuitable causes abstentions rather than real changes and this is what the selection committees are watching for. Playing safe, then, with identikit family man candidates is an increasing trend with both the main parties. The Liberals play around a bit more, matching Sikh candidates to predominantly middle class constituencies with large Indian representation like Sheffield, Hallam; or Jewish candidates in predominantly Jewish areas like Hampstead or Finchley. They used to tend to put up with more colourful characters than the other two parties; though a more cautious pattern is emerging hand in hand with greater electoral success.

Colourful characters, according to Marcus Lipton, who is one himself, are fewer in the House than ever before. The loss of Harry Legge Bourke and Gerald Nabarro who died in 1973, and the resignation of Enoch Powell have decreased the colour of the House still further. The grey men come and go as surely they have always done so, though perhaps not two by two as they do now. Each typical Tory and his typical Labour pair, middle class, red brick University and Grammar School educated marching down the lobbies are indistinguishable up to the point of Aye and No.

It is the remarkable similarity between so many Members of both Government and Opposition parties that is now so striking. One must look close indeed at the newer Members to tell them apart. Nowadays, like the sexes, Labour and Tory back-benchers look much the same from behind.

From the front, there are still some discernible differences.

The Tory MPs are substantially better looking and are certainly taller on the whole. The latter characteristic may have a great deal to do with nutrition and class among the older Members. As one Labour Member said: 'A lot of our fellows grew up in the thirties in unemployed families. They didn't get enough to eat.' Even Labour men who are middle class and middle aged now could have come from poorer homes and suffered from a lack of body building foods before the introduction of school milk. The preponderance of good looks must, however, have another explanation. No one could actually propose the argument that the upper classes are better looking than the working classes. Great beauties have often risen, like Sophia Loren, from the slums, and the County has produced many a crop of horse-faced fillies. No, the answer to the prettiness of the Tory men must lie with the great influence of the Tory ladies on the selection committees.

Bill Elliott tells an anecdote in support of this theory. He sent a brilliant candidate for selection to a certain constituency party. Considering that the man had all the qualities necessary to make an excellent MP and also, says Elliott, 'was ministerial material' (something well worth watching for) he gave him an excellent commendation. Soon after the constituency Chairman was on the telephone asking why such an emphatic commendation had been given. When told why he replied that that was all very well but the candidate was 'such a damn plain fellow'.

Indeed, charm if not good looks are an asset in a Parliamentary candidate. The Labour Party is not without its handsome men. The Liberal Party during the 1959 to 1964 period ran a fine string of pretty fellows to the hustings. Strangely the women of politics are on the whole not as lovely to look at as the men. There are probably more attractive looking women on the Labour benches than on the Tory ones. This may be because pretty girls are as unpopular with Tory ladies as handsome men are popular, or perhaps it is because, as William Elliott says, 'Prettiness does not go with politics'.

It is worth examining the reasons why women — although roughly 50 per cent of the population and the electorate — are so poorly represented in the House. The largest number of women ever elected was 29 in 1964. In 1966 there were 26 women elected and by the end of the 1970–74 Parliament there were 27 women in the House. In 1974, when more women stood for Parliament than on any previous occasion, only 25 were elected.

The reasons are several. In the first place women do not come forward for selection in the same numbers as men. When they do they are irrevocably middle class, educated women. Then there is the plain fact that when they do come forward, women find it harder to get selected than men, and particularly find it harder to get selected for the winnable constituencies.

There is evidence that times are changing. In the first place women are getting elected younger. Although the average age of women Members in the last House, at 57, came considerably higher than the bulge in the graph for Members' total ages, women candidates seem to be getting selected at an earlier age than in the past. Many of the previous women Membership of the Commons seem to have entered the House in their forties or even later. Recently young, even glamorous women seem to be having a go at what must until recently have seemed like a blue stocking preserve.

When I fought my first election in 1966 I was the youngest woman candidate at the age of 25. Four years later Bernadette Devlin careered into Parliament at the age of 21. Women have not looked back since. When Margo MacDonald was elected in the 1973 Glasgow Govan by-election for an all too short time, her blonde good looks were a sign that women with political ambition need no longer pretend to be plain and worthy in order to get either nomination or votes. Some kind of revolution in attitudes had been taking place and perhaps the much maligned Bernadette Devlin (now Macalisky) had much to do with it thanks to her refusal to compromise. No chignon, black dresses or pearls for her. So the rest of us could relax and throw off our middle aged disguise. Flowing tresses were seen at the hustings in 1974. Prettiness was going with politics after all. And why not? The voters seemed to enjoy it. One man told me: 'I'm going right home to tell my wife to vote for you because I fancy you.' Anne Mallalieu, pretty blonde Labour candidate, was told: 'You're the only red I want to see in my bed.' So much for the fun of the fair. Women certainly did not disgrace themselves at the polls, and their own sex was voting for them especially.

The mileage made by women during the late sixties also owes much to the sometimes stident calls of Women's Lib. Not only were women voters more aware of a solidarity as women but the subtle suggestion that women were perhaps unacceptable to selection committees could no longer be made without embarrassment. Moreover, women themselves were beginning to hustle for women. By-election wins by women were also an indication that the voters were not selecting against the female sex. So why should the selectors?

Caution is, however, hard to disperse. The Liberals took a correct step when they announced that every selection meeting should consider at least one woman on its short list. Some constituencies actually expressed a preference for a woman candidate: women, after all, get more attention than men from the media. The bore of being asked to be a statutory woman at every selection meeting then fell to the more noticeable women prospectives in 1974. But the fact that Liberals ran forty women on the hustings, as did Labour that February suggests that once the selection meeting sees a woman, they often overcome their theoretical objections and she runs away with the nomination.

This fact was shown to be true in much darker days for women than the seventies. Reg Underhill tells of an occasion when his efforts to persuade the Coventry Labour Party to consider a woman. They refused, yet at their selection conference failed to select anyone. Second time round they agreed to consider Underhill's woman nominee. They selected her and she became Elaine Burton, MP, now Baroness Burton.

The Conservative Party, as ever, presents the hardest task for women. Often Conservative women seem to have spent long periods in local government, sometimes as much as twenty years before getting selected for winnable Parliamentary seats. The election of Linda Chalker, aged 31, and a divorcee

48

to boot in 1974 was the first definite sign that things were looking up for Tory women, though perhaps the easy win by the attractive Mrs. Sally Oppenheim with no previous experience in 1970 was the thin end of the wedge. But the Conservative Party still put up fewer women candidates (33) in 1974 than did Labour (40) or Liberal (40).

Once elected women find it easy to distinguish themselves and no doubt further help to the cause of feminism has come from the success in office of competent women like Barbara Castle, Shirley Williams, Margaret Thatcher. Unfortunately, the fact that women are more easily noticeable than men also shows up the silly ones as being more silly than the average male fool. But that is one of the hazards.

To a degree women have to be that bit better still than their male counterpart to get the nomination. However they tend to acquire a stronger hold on their constituencies in terms of personal support more easily. Performance on the hustings indicates an advantage for women candidates. Certainly Liberal women did better on the whole in 1974 (getting 21·4 per cent of the vote) than Liberals as a whole (19·3 per cent). There are still obstacles in their path in spite of the improved climate and the principle one is the stumbling block of marriage, children and the traditional role of women in the home. Many women do not feel able to enter Parliamentary politics until their children are of a reasonable age. This is to their credit. But there is a reasonable school of thought which says that labour in the home can be divided and that if men can enter politics as fathers, then women as mothers should not find more difficulty. The fact is that both sexes have difficulty with their family obligations once they have entered Parliament but the structure of society makes a woman's burden worse.

Selection committees are bound to consider this and do. But not only if the child-minder is the mother. I sat through one selection meeting in which one of the candidates, male having given his profession as house husband had to answer questions about whether his duties towards his two children would be in any way neglected as a result of his adoption, and also what would happen to them if he was elected.

If sex, race and status counts or is alleged to count with the voters how much does the individual matter? What exactly is the factor of the personal vote? 'Good candidates,' according to Bill Elliott, 'rarely put up the votes in any noticeable way.' And that in spite of all the care taken by selectors. Although many candidates and Members of Parliament like to flatter themselves that they have a personal vote it is unlikely that they can count more than a hundred or so in a normal electoral situation as being for them and them alone. People vote for parties. And against policies. Even a Member of the Mafia with the right colour rosette could find himself elected on a party ticket. A waxwork could do the same. But in exceptional situations a personal vote can suddenly materialise. In 1970 Stephen Davies, having been asked to stand down by his local party for Merthyr Tydfil, which he had represented since 1934, on the grounds that at 84 he was too old, refused the official nomination, stood as Independent and was elected. He held the seat until his death in 1972 whereupon the constituency returned a Labour Member in the by-election in spite of the fact that an S. O. Davies faction candidate was standing.

Likewise, Dick Taverne held on to his seat of Lincoln in the by-election brought about by his own resignation which itself was the result of his own party disowning him over his Common Market views. He held on with a decreased majority in 1974. Yet other Taverne Democratic Labour candidates have had no success.

Ted Milne, similarly refusing the nomination in his constituency of Blythe over some remarks he had made about corruption in the Labour Party, also stood as an Independent in 1974 and was likewise returned against the official candidate.

Freak by-election results are often brought about by the heavy reneging of personal votes away from the party of the deceased Member and towards some new personality or party. The Ely by-election in which Clement Freud was elected after the death of the well known and colourful Harry Legge Bourke —always a rebel on the Tory back-benches—was one such. The fact that Freud increased his majority in 1974 where other Liberal by-election victors lost out supports this view. Similarly Jeremy Thorpe's immense personal appeal in the 1974 General Election helped to turn a marginal of a few hundred votes into a 35,000 majority, and in spite of boundary changes that could have lost him the seat by around 19,000 votes.

A mixture of good personality and devotion to constituency affairs can help to establish a Member in the minds and hearts of the constituents. As Bill Elliott says, 'After a long time people perhaps begin to feel that the Member has a right to the seat.' But this is a benefit of time which is a property of the more stable communities. In urban or suburban seats a Member will need to be a national figure for any 'personal' effect to apply. But even then, in a massive turn around against the holder's party, any prominent figure in a relatively marginal seat would be less likely to survive in the urban than in country areas. The reason is that urban and suburban constituencies, particularly those around London, tend to have a large element of mobility in the population. In outer London as much as one-sixth of the electorate can change per year. In ten years it is possible for as much as two-thirds of a Member's supporters to move away and there is no guarantee that they would be replaced by voters with the same party affiliations.

Population mobility is one factor which helps towards the dominance of the party affiliation in voting patterns. Over the past decade or so both mobility and party ticket voting have become more prevalent. Thus even a Member with a good record can be heartlessly cast out and replaced by a less effective Member of another party. Likewise, even a really bad MP can retain his seat because the voters' desire to elect a particular party to Government, or keep another party out, is more powerful than the desire to elect a good MP.

If this is a sad evidence of the fact that voters care more about the colour of government that the quality of Parliament, then 1974 brought indications of a change of heart. The personal factor was here in evidence, confounding the swingometers already confused by the disrupting effect of nation-wide boundary changes. Although party voting was still a dominant factor, people were on the whole more generous to individuals as they were to the smaller parties. Hence some Members increased their majorities where they should have lost their seats, and indeed where others in comparable situations did lose. Volatility was a popular phrase applied to the electorate by experts. The truth was that in the general disaffection with party politics, national figures or well-known individuals exerted a personal pull far greater than under 'normal' conditions, where hard line clear-cut party alignments push personality into second place.

The ordinary, good or even exceptional candidate, if unknown, cannot compete with a well-known personality or even with the appeal of the party ticket. In a General Election most candidates tend to produce a result that conforms to a national swing. However, a bad candidate or an unpopular Member can produce a more drastic effect — perhaps because people are more vehement when against than for something. Local issues and the association of a candidate with them can also cause dramatic and anomalous results. The election of Stephen Ross at the Isle of Wight in February 1974 was a case in point: from third place in 1970 Ross put on over twenty thousand votes and was elected with a majority of 7,766. Here the local Member Mark Woodnutt's association with a very unpopular local project was the undoubted cause.

Justly or unjustly, a sitting Member's connections with anything unsavoury, from something as innocent as a dipsomaniac wife, to a call-girl, a tax fiddle or a really serious smell of corruption can lose him votes or even his seat. An opposing candidate can do more badly than average for less sinister reasons.

One Conservative MP tells an illustrative tale about a post-war Churchill candidate, who although a highly decorated fighter-pilot, was new to politics and in particular to the hustings. Nevertheless he became adopted for a tough industrial seat in the North. The great Labour landslide of 1945 was not anticipated at the time of his adoption and it was therefore something of a shock to the brave fighter-pilot when he received his first baptism of heckling. Having braved war in the air he was unable to brave battle at the hustings: after a few rough meetings the poor man lost his nerve and kept off stage for the remainder of the campaign. This example of hopelessly bad candidature was well endorsed by the worse than abysmal result; and that this only goes to prove that bad candidates lose more votes than good ones can possibly gain.

The qualities acceptable in safe seats are not necessarily the same as those in a marginal seat. The loss of a few hundred votes in a safe seat with a majority of ten thousand go relatively unnoticed. Problems like not being able to render oneself coherent in public, looking ugly on telly, and even having the wrong sort of wife — for instance one that drinks or dresses badly — are tolerable.

There is always the chance that someone who is classed as a poor candidate can make a very good MP. One Labour Member who as a candidate was relatively unpresentable, and a poor speaker is now such a devoted constituency Member that he holds three surgeries a week. Unfortunately there are more examples of the converse.

How Does Education Count?

As far as qualifications and proven ability is concerned, the House is well endowed. Brian Walden says: 'We have a better quality of Member than any other representative House in the world.' Certainly there is an increasing emphasis on educational and professional qualifications among the candidates being selected. Rightly or wrongly, selection committees consider that an educated Member is better than one that left school at 15.

In the 1966–70 Parliament 28 per cent of MPs left school at 15.* Most of these were Labour. But it is interesting to note that the proportion was greater for the older age groups than the younger ones: 12 per cent were under 40; 26 per cent were 40–60 and 45 per cent were 60 plus. Eighteen Members of the

* A survey carried out on health and work in the House of Commons on behalf of the British Heart Foundation.

1964–70 Labour Cabinet came into this educational category.

The Labour Party is most concerned to raise the educational standard of its candidates. It would be unfair to say that education has any real bearing on a man's ability to do his job and everyone knows that academic qualifications are meaningless without experience. A degree helps one to think problems through with analytical methodology. It does not necessarily help him to be any better at his job, whatever that may be unless analytical thinking is a major aspect of the job. Education is getting a bad name because of the standards it fails to reach. Nevertheless its superficial manifestations are much revered. Not least at the Amalgamated Union of Engineering Workers, which is busy testing all its prospective candidates for their ability to read, write and speak.

Reg Underhill admits 'a higher educational standard amongst candidates is desirable'. This act of subscription to the great education farce is a part of the general trend towards meritocracy, started by Harold Wilson. It is true that the Labour Party wants to better educational standards and we can all argue about the best method of doing that. But there is something wrong with a system in which only the educated can aspire to a place in Parliament. If eighteen Labour Ministers can do their thing without even a GCE 'O' Level, should we reject as a candidate someone who happens not to be able to read or write? The answer in a competitive world is probably yes.

The private secretary to a Labour Minister told me that he had to draft even the correspondence for his boss, who could barely read or write. MPs have to be able to read reports and papers, draft questions, write letters to constituents and to the local press. It is one thing to win a seat with rabble-rousing oratory but another to hold it. As for holding office — a basic standard of literary ability is essential.

The AUEW whose share of Members in the House is increasing examines for every aspect of candidature. The process as explained to me by Brother Ernest Roberts, the Assistant General Secretary was as follows: to get sponsorship a candidate must be put forward by one of the 2,750 branches of the

Union. About two hundred nominations go through to the next stage. The Union can finance as many as one candidate per 30,000 members — and there is a total of about 900,000 members altogether. This means that a total of 30 members can be accepted for candidature. About 100 go through for final selection.

There are currently 21 AUE sponsored members in the House. Three more AUE candidates have been adopted for safe Labour seats which will become vacant at the next General Election. Thus in addition to the MPs there are 100 nominees to be considered. These all go for selection interviews of the most elaborate kind.

The Union takes all the nominees to a hotel for the week-end, presents them with a written paper, and with various oral tests helped along by tough questioning from newspaper correspondents and the existing AUE sponsored MPs. Even a local audience of hecklers consisting of young Conservatives and any other political provocationists that can be raked up by newspaper advertisements in the district, is invited in.

The result is that a number of nominees are finally considered to have 'passed' and become Union-sponsored candidates. These, then, need to be selected by constituency associations and adopted as candidates before they can actually get anywhere. The AUE is, however, increasing its share of the Trade Union Membership in the House. Perhaps this is related to the rigorous selection procedures. The trend towards written and oral examination of potential candidates is likely to spread to other Unions. It is certainly being encouraged by Transport House.

Such is the confidence of the two main parties that their candidates will be elected that grooming and training are never wasted. The smaller parties have to rely more on natural ability in their candidates. But even the Liberals hold week-end schools and teach TV techniques. The Welsh Nationalists for instance will put up anyone who is willing to stand and who believes in self-government for Wales. There are other criteria; but policy on other matters is never a deciding factor in selection. Luckily the Nationalists have attracted highly educated candidates. Similarly, the Liberals have a galaxy of illustrious personalities among their candidates.

Communist candidates are usually admired for their fluency. When it is decided to contest a seat, however, the CP is not trying to win so much as make a point. As a representative of the party told me, 'We stand when there is someone whose policies we particularly oppose contesting the seat. If the local party agree to fight and we can find a candidate we fight. We would,' he said, 'for instance, oppose Robert Carr because he brought in the Industrial Relations Act.'

Not all the people who stand for Parliament do so because they believe they will be elected. Liberals, Nationalists and most Independents stand in order to give a platform to their politics. To be elected is not necessarily the objective. To be heard is the main thing. Candidates are, in this case, better if they are fluent, have oratorical powers, know their facts and how to put them over. Being able to read or write, knowing how Parliament works or making promises to the electors are not important for this type of candidate.

In contrast, the main party candidate must know his party policy, must stand on it, defend it, outline areas of disagreement, be loyal to his leaders and promise the world to his voters. He is already on the treadmill of subjugation to the party machine. Whatever the qualities he has he can be sure that he is in a small way the pawn of king makers. He has been chosen to represent a party. From this point on he begins to know, whether he is elected or not, what it will be like to be an MP; to be answerable to the many different people to whom he owes his political chance.

Is Honesty the Best Policy?

Whatever the differences between parties and between selectors and the men they select, all constituency associations and all voters look in their candidates for one special quality — honesty. After making the incumbent stand on his head; compromise his personal opinions with those of the party; make all manner of promises such as to live in the constituency; vote this way and that on emotional issues; and canvass three nights a week before getting elected, they ask for honesty. How right they are. Without a spark of honesty at this stage no man could survive the trials and temptations which, for any would-be MP, lie ahead.

3

A CALL TO ARMS

Elections are the living demonstration of democracy at work. But to the electors they are something of a bore. Canvassers knock doors at dinner-time or during a favourite TV programme: party political broadcasts bore away on all channels: TV, radio and the newspapers are riveted by news discussion, reports of political abuse and swings of the national opinion polls: loudspeakers touring council estates waken shift workers and children: election literature flows through the letter-box: on top of all this one has to find time to vote; or else be dragged to the polling station willy-nilly by a team of knockers-up.

Only the politicians really enjoy elections. They show off. This is their biggest opportunity to be listened to. Public meetings, open-air speeches, car cavalcades, abusing opponents, all done with gusto replace the dull business of everyday politics. Even the most insignificant politician can make a stir with a well-timed ribaldry. Litigation is threatened. Leaflets are printed and words fly faster than the rain in February. Elections are a fight: and politicians and their immediate supporters love it.

There are exceptions. Some of the older Members find elections tiring or tedious. Some politicians lack the touch of theatre required for such public exposure: some simply lack, like Alec Douglas Home, the common touch.

For the less well off politicians elections are a considerable expense. For most candidates, the election period is two and a half or three weeks away from their livelihood. MPs used to feel particular hardship especially if thrown out: Parliamentary salaries traditionally stop from the day Parliament is dissolved until the day the Members are sworn in once more for the new one. But the recent Boyle report on Members' Pay and Conditions changed all that and Members will not only be paid for the election period, but if they lose their seats, for three months afterwards as well.

Some politicians dislike elections because of shyness. Reginald Maudling is one who visibly disliked campaigning. Quiet introverted people are not in the majority in politics. The few that there are, are at a severe disadvantage during electioneering. There are some candidates who are better on a platform and some who are better shaking hands with people on the doorstep. There are also a lucky few who are good at both and an unlucky minority who are good at neither.

The reason why most politicians enjoy the general scrummage of the election is the very same reason others hate it. Elections are the point where the politician really comes into close contact with people, at their roughest, most critical, and most politically activated.

Press and TV coverage heightens political side-taking among the electors. All the barriers are down: the candidate is at last face to face with real live people who smile, laugh, scowl, jeer, cheer or pointedly ignore him. To the tender soul, all this is pure hell. To the others it is a lark.

What Are the Techniques of Electioneering?

The technique of electioneering is often a question of personal preferences for the candidate. Conditions however play an important part in determining the style of the campaign. Sitting Members with large majorities play things cool. Those contending try to hot the campaign up. During the Brighton Pavilion by-election, which I fought as a Liberal in 1969, this was the case. Worse, the press began all their stories with the words: 'It is a foregone conclusion that the Conservatives will win . . .' However glowing the article in favour of Opposition candidates, this sort of treatment tends to render the campaign something of a non event contest for second place. In such a case, the candidate for the entrenched party need hardly bother to be seen in the streets, far less on the doorsteps: it is up to the other candidates to turn a foregone conclusion into an election.

The more marginal the constituency, the more active all candidates have to be. Most candidates work quite hard in any case. An average daily schedule could look something like this:

6.00 or 7.00 a.m.	Rise and shine.
7.00 or 8.00 a.m.	Tour of stations and bus stops talking to commuters (frankly a ridiculous idea). Commuters feel no more like talking than the candidate but agents seem to think the operation shows willing if nothing else).
9.00 a.m.	Breakfast — they need it. Check papers.
9.30 a.m.	Press conference or speech preparation.
10.00 a.m.	Photocall for evening papers.
10.30 a.m.	Talking to shoppers in the local market.
12 noon	Hustings in the market square or car tour.
12.30 p.m.	Lunch — another public occasion quite possibly: pub or restaurant.
1.30 p.m.	The experienced candidate has a rest. The others go out canvassing an hour earlier.
2.30 p.m.	Canvassing housing estates.
3.30 p.m.	Talking to mums outside the schools.
4.00 p.m.	Filming with TV camera team (anything up to an hour filming for three minutes on the screen) or photocall for national papers.
5.00 p.m.	Quick tour in loud speaker car of major railway stations to blast propaganda at the commuters again.
6.00 p.m.	Short rest.
6.30 p.m.	Answering correspondence, writing last minute speeches.
7.00 p.m.	First meeting of the evening. For a rural candidate these are particularly important and there may have to be two or three in different centres every night. Otherwise more doorstepping.

9.30 p.m.   Mercifully not much more that can be done
with the electors but organisation may need
supervision. Chats with the agent and staff
over dinner can easily take up to 11.00 p.m.
or later.

This pattern by no means includes all the variables. Local
problems blow up suddenly during an election campaign. Details may need to be swotted up during a fast car drive between
meetings. Meetings themselves often in large constituencies
overlap and have to be hotted up by other speakers while the
candidate rushes madly across country from the previous as-
sembly. The growth of the importance of media also takes its
toll during the day: press, radio and TV interviews take up an
alarming amount of the time that should really be spent talking
directly to the electors.

Reporters often influence the course of the campaign by
setting off sparring between the candidates. Something said
by one candidate at a press conference is repeated by pressmen,
rushing hot-foot to the next in the hope of stirring up copy.
Pressmen can even invent a bone of contention for the candidates to toss about amongst each other for a few days. With
luck all the old standbys of accusations, inflammatory replies
and libel suit can be stirred up, by a reporter's seemingly innocent question. This is news manufactured and real politics
ignored.

Talking to the people should come high on any candidate's
list of priorities. But most candidates have to contemplate the
prospect of trying to talk to anything between sixty thousand
and a hundred thousand people during the course of three
weeks. This unimaginable feat is rarely attempted seriously but
some candidates give a creditable appearance of doing their
best. American tactics have crept into the style of a number of
the trendier Tory candidates in recent years: and at every by-
election the nation is bored by TV interviews with the candidate who is filmed leaping over garden fences. Electors, fished
out by the candidates aides stand, hands outstretched, waiting
for their split-second contact with the flying candidate.

Most of these attempts are pure public relations. A candidate tears up a suitably prepared street under the lens of the camera only to sink back into the passenger seat of the loudspeaker car a few minutes later. Nevertheless the televised impression given to the electors is that the candidate wants to meet them all; even if it is hardly long enough to register any complaints.

Real doorstep work is part of the business of conversion which should really be carried out between elections by dutiful party hacks. Certain kinds of candidate need to be introduced to their public as infrequently as possible largely because they are not at their best — to put it kindly — in face to face contact. Unlovely candidates are no better on TV either, but there is always radio, the loudspeaker car, the waning opportunities for platform oratory, or the smart comment in the press.

With all the interruptions that take place during an election campaign most candidates meet no more than a comparative handful of their constituents during the course of it. By-elections are different. During a General Election ordinary candidates have fewer interruptions in the way of national media men but the media play an even stronger part in separating the candidate from the electors. Frequently the candidate knocks on a door to be told that his or her party political spokesman has or is at that moment saying specific things on the television. Whether the candidate agrees or not he has little chance of putting a local interpretation onto the sayings of his party nationally. As an individual he is very much dwarfed by the national discussions of various issues which take the battle into zones over which he has little control. If there was one thing that Julian Amery and I were agreed about during the course of the Brighton Pavilion by-election, it was as he said to me in the Mayor's Parlour that 'by-elections give one the opportunity to play things one's own way'. For individualists — and politicians tend to be so — a by-election is the opportunity to be one's own General. In a General Election one must be content to be a mere Sergeant. But then much of the burden is borne nationally too and the responsibility for success or failure rests squarely at the centre.

62

As far as being known by the constituents is concerned, the sitting Members have a definite advantage. A new candidate or for that matter any Opposition candidate will suffer from a touch of 'better the devil you know' philosophy among the electors. To nullify the MPs advantage the challenger must either be a national figure or have as his opponent someone who has fallen from favour. Both these conditions are rare.

Publicity and the Party Machine

Since the opportunities to meet the constituents are few, every bit of personal publicity the candidate can get counts towards getting himself across. Everything else depends upon the effect his party is having on the mass media. Most of all the candidate is the victim of the party system. He is as powerless as the electors to comment upon or resist the lugubrious force of the press and TV campaigns as perpetrated by his Party's leaders and the admass men who guide their movements through the opinion poll towards the final verdict.

Thus the help given to a candidate by his Party's central organisation at a local level is a crucial factor for competitiveness. In order to see how the central organisation can be of assistance let us first look at the basic requirements which any party organiser up from agent level would consider absolutely necessary to the successful conduct of an election campaign.

In the first place the constituency party must be in good shape. Ideally, canvassing and various activation programmes should have been in operation in the interim period. Constituency party membership should be at least one-fifth of the number of votes required to win the seat. There should be a permanently resident agent, preferably well paid, and a fine team of willing workers who will rip into action at the flick of a finger and thumb once the dissolution is declared. The constituency party should have a sizable income, preferably at least five thousand a year.

Most candidates who have fought derelict or hopeless constituencies would find the above list hysterically funny. This means Liberals, Nationalists and Independents. But there are many Labour Party candidates, even many who are currently MPs who regard these qualifications for success as well beyond their reach. The Conservative Party, on the other hand, is the one which sets this particular standard: and it is the aim of every candidate who believes that elections are won through organisation to imitate their superb example.

For a period after the legendary Orpington by-election the Liberal Party became obsessed with organisation. Eric Lubbock (now Lord Avebury) had as his agent in Orpington, Pratrap Chitnis, who later was to become Head of the Liberal Party Organisation (on Jeremy Thorpe's election to the leadership).

Chitnis has a reputation as a superb organiser: his cool blend of cynicism with gambler's nerve would be an invaluable asset to any candidate. The pattern of the growth of the party organisation at Orpington was blue-printed and every Liberal Organisation in the country strained to copy it. One vital ingredient was missing for most of them and that was timing. Orpington was won on the crest of the wave for Liberalism. The Macmillan Government was tottering and not everyone wanted Harold Wilson's magic recipe for the white hot technological revolution. Socialism was and clearly still is a dirty word in Orpington and the expanding, property conscious, middle class areas like it. It was a combination of many factors of which organisation was only a part which helped the winsome Mr. Lubbock into Parliament. But whatever the other factors, the seat would not have been won in this way had it not been for the organisation.

Likewise at Sutton and Cheam in 1972, the thundering by-election victory for Liberals was a comment on the success of a six-months slog at community politics masterminded by Trevor Jones.

Politics is indeed a game for opportunists: and any opportunist worth his salt is ready and waiting to grasp what comes along. Very few constituency parties prepare themselves adequately for the swing in the tide. For the two big parties this is less important, the tide goes their way sooner or later: even so, their clear dependence on the size of the swing shows in many cases that real between election organisation is lacking except of course in the Tory Party.

To a certain extent the nature of parties dictates the type of organisation they develop. Conservatives have a rather social set-up: recruitment of a steady membership benefits from recurrent social occasions where people can be lured into little organisational roles or encouraged to undertake small duties. In contrast the Labour Party does not work this way: its strength lies in its loyal support which is largely working class based. The most important time for Labour is during the latter stages of the election campaign, significantly in the evening of polling day when the most important task of the campaign for the party is carried out. Labour voters have often to be dragged 'kicking and screaming' to the polls. Knocking-up is therefore the constituency Labour Party forte. Its importance is shown by the fact that a Labour win corresponds to a high poll (see figures for 1964, 1966 and 1974 elections) as compared with substantially lower polls when they lose. This is also the case for the Liberal Party. A 43 per cent poll at Brighton Pavilion lost me my deposit. It gave Labour a vote worth only a quarter of its 1966 figure. In February 1974 a 78·4 per cent poll nationally gave Liberals over six million votes and Labour the edge in Parliament.

In all organisations numbers win in the end: the smaller parties lose out unless they have an extraordinary tidal swing in their favour. At the start of the Brighton campaign I had a Liberal constituency party totalling ten people. By the end I had fifty regular helpers. The local Conservatives had a membership of thousands. But the rules can be broken. Gwynfor Evans, the Welsh Nationalist, the first Nationalist elected in the recent wave, succeeded because of one of those mysterious political tidal waves that fortunately occur every now and again to frighten the pollsters and pundits and bring a breath of hope into the whole boringly predictable business. The local Nationalist Party was certainly not small in this case but it hardly had the poll knocking powers that a crack organisation of the kind used in Orpington can have. Having done a week's door stepping in that campaign I can say, however, that the political change had happened already in the minds of the people before any organisation got to work. The high level of Liberal support nationally in February 1974 was also due to the electorate's mood more than to any organisational readiness.

Important though the local party organisation is in clinching the certainty of any result there are other factors not so frequently talked about. Money is an impressive aid to the winning of seats. For this reason the system of limitation of election expenses has been brought in in order to give those who cannot spend lavishly an opportunity to compete fairly with those who, given the chance, would spare no expense. Having fought three elections on £500 each I can safely say that £1,000 does not buy much. Even the deposit for many Liberals has to be scraped out of similarly meagre sums or the pockets of the local people — themselves very rarely prosperous in any way. Constituency Labour Parties are similarly poor but at least have at their back the substantial sums claimed by the national organisation from the coffers of the Trade Unions. The Labour Party has a guaranteed income which, in spite of local poverty of resources, give it a roaring start over the Liberals and the Nationalists. The Conservatives have it both ways and frequently have large numbers of prosperous people contributing sizable sums locally: this quite apart from the substantial donations received by Central Office from industry and commerce.

Much good this money may do them, it might be thought, once election expenses are being counted: but as every shrewd campaigner knows there are ways and means around that problem and declared expenses are often as little as a quarter of the actual amount spent. At least it may be said the system keeps the differences down to a smaller amount than they would normally be if the richer local parties spent what they could comfortably afford. There is certainly a case for the allowable amounts to be increased. Printing costs and almost every other form of expense has risen wildly since the last amount was fixed. But even if the level were raised there would still be constituency parties who could raise no more than a meagre £500.

It is arguable that money counts: but almost all successful perpetrators of political coups like the Orpington by-election will admit that they spent plenty of money and that it undoubtedly helped. In the cases where the money is not available locally this sort of advantage has to be provided centrally. A trained agent and numerous experienced organisers is one of the assets Conservative Central Office supplies to its by-election candidates. In General Elections these resources are not available for most candidates. Literature, posters and the manifesto are amongst the other assistance provided centrally by all parties, but usually at a cost to the local organisation except in special circumstances.

The value of these aids is dubious. More likely they are a part of the moral support that the central organisation needs to offer to keep the local party to heel in harder times. Posters, for example, are a very popular form of election time publicity. Window bills and car stickers are the more usual form but central organisations do provide and pay for hoardings in certain cases. For instance, the Labour Party provided hoarding sites and posters for its hard-pressed marginals in the 1970 campaign. However, a delightful indication that posters may not be all they are cracked up to be came when Hampstead, a seat held between 1966 and 1970 by Ben Whittaker for Labour with a margin of 2,253 votes and almost bound to be lost with even a slight swing was refused the Transport House posters. 'Hampstead,' says Whittaker, 'is not one of Transport House's favourite constituency Labour Parties.' The seat was, however, lost with a swing of only 2·5 per cent, one of the smallest in the country. Posters, it may be argued, could have saved the seat.

Training and the Grooming for Battle

The help given to candidates by their central party organisations goes further than the financial and material aids supplied during the campaign itself. The preparation of candidates for their big chance goes on to a varying extent in the preceding months and years. The preparative aids vary in extent from the supply of policy material to extensive training courses in every aspect of candidature. Bearing in mind that the candidate is a potential MP, the training may in some cases extend to an actual preparation for the work to be done once the candidate is the elected Member.

One organisation which devotes itself to the thorough training of its candidates for their duties to come is the Amalgamated Union of Engineering Workers. A powerful and growing body of about nine hundred thousand members, the AUEW has a most rigorous selection and training procedure for its sponsored candidates of any section of the Labour Party and certainly of any organisation selecting Parliamentary candidates in Britain. Once its candidates are on the sponsored list the process of grooming them for office begins. The AUEW starts with a premiss that an organisation such as the Tory Party does not need, which is that the grooming process needs to be started at the first base-line. Whereas the Conservative Party and also the Liberal Party confine themselves to limited television training and an annual or bi-annual week-end candidates' school, the AUEW takes its candidates away regularly for training in such activities as writing letters to the local press, answering questions at a public meeting and dealing with a press conference. The leader of the Party, and Labour Shadow Ministers (or Ministers as the case may be) attend these schools and talk to candidates about their style and approach. Lectures are given on speech construction and the presentation of policy.

From what I remember of Liberal Party week-end candidates' schools, these were something of a social occasion. I found my colleagues a thoroughly congenial bunch and we spent some riotous week-ends. We formed pressure groups for getting our own way in the party and we occasionally had useful discussions on policy aspects. Though these occasions may have helped to develop the fine areas of political opinion on certain topical subjects, they were not strictly valuable in training us for any future aspect of political life other than perhaps our relationships within our own group as a 'future' Parliamentary Liberal Party.

One of the most valuable forcing periods for political education for the young politician or the new candidate occurs annually at the party conferences. Party members of all parties may sometimes ask themselves why the party goes to the expense of putting on this elaborate show once a year at the slag end of the silly season. The fact that in the Liberal Party at least the decline in conference attendance tends to follow the decline in political power suggests that politics is a major reason for attending conferences.

For the people who attend conferences, the prospect of a mighty binge mixed with their political roadshow is clearly inviting enough to make it worth taking a week's holiday. The party rank and file get a chance to mingle with the great or at least the famous and often enough to bend their ear. For the up and coming candidate there is likewise an opportunity to mingle, grind axes, tout for constituencies, pick up hints from the more experienced, and get into the limelight and show what they can do. Audiences at party conferences run into thousands and are certainly the best practice any young orator can get. Big audiences otherwise are a thing of the past, but there is immense value for a candidate in getting the feel of a reasonably sophisticated political audience, even if the biggest likely to be mustered at election time is two or three hundred.

Changing Peoples Minds — What Chance?

Although public meetings are waning in popularity in favour of television politics, oratory is still the real stuff of politics. Those who can and even those who can't turn an audience in the palm of their hand are usually excited and elated by speech-making. Public speaking may be a technique which can be learned but true oratory is born. A technician's speech is too clearly recognisable for what it is: an orator has his audience's emotions under control. Emotion is an essential part of speaking to a live audience and it is only too sadly lacking in the medium of TV. Great words spoken on TV lack even the magic of those emerging from the infinitely more dramatic medium of radio. But live stage is best: the curious relationship between speaker and audience is broken once they are physically isolated from each other.

One of the reasons why so many politicians enjoy elections, particularly the hustings and the village hall, is that the sense of power they get by tapping the emotional potential of live audiences is more rewarding than any slick verbage in Parliament or on TV. The reaction they get is what politics is all about.

It is at the live meeting more than at any other time that the politician has the opportunity to change people's minds. What is said, how it is said and the emotions it evokes are the key to conversion. Floating voters often go to public meetings to have their minds made up for them. I did it myself in 1970. I have had genuinely undecided electors question me at my own meetings. Often one factor is enough to alienate the floater or else to bag him. A question on comprehensive schools, taxation, or even foreign affairs is all that he wants answered before making up his mind. If this is the case the candidate has a fifty-fifty chance of getting the vote or losing it. Only when the floater is more generally undecided, on a matter of principle or wider policy issues does oratory do the trick. That it can do so I am convinced: sometimes for as vague a reason as the integrity of the candidate — the fact that the audience feels he genuinely cares. But these instances are rare. They do not win elections, but they can help to when electors are in genuine doubt.

It is possible that voters in marginal constituencies under conditions likely to give a swing towards the Opposition Party, give more careful consideration to their vote than in non-marginals. In the latter, the foregone conclusion philosophy tends to encourage the preponderance of present voting habits amongst the voters. It could be that, as figures tend to show, polls in non-marginals are often markedly lower than in marginals, the undecided tending to abstain. In a marginal seat that has a strong chance of changing hands, electors who might normally feel apathetic about registering their opposition vote, go to the polls with the definite impression that their vote may count.

The two important lessons to be learned by any candidate in any seat from this observation are: (1) that voters like to feel their vote could have an effect on the final result, not only in their constituency but also nationally; and (2) that in a marginal situation there are probably more floating voters in a potentially activable condition. The ability to give the impression that he can win — or retain as the case may be, the seat at such a time is then vital in the process of bringing favourably disposed floaters over to his way of thinking; then galvanising them into enough feeling of urgency to get them to the polling station.

Candidates in marginal seats should therefore be fighters and able to give the impression that they believe in themselves. As far as most selection procedures go it is probably hit and miss that this sort of consideration is given any importance.

Again, rather more for the marginal candidates than for the safe seat people, the election will cause a fair amount of nervous strain. The pattern of activity rises to a peak of importance immediately before the last week-end of the campaign. This is the period when most electors seem to finally make up their minds about which way to vote. Rumour has it that this last Sunday of the campaign is the one on which husband and wife sit down together over a nice cup of something and read through their election addresses. Cynics will doubt that election addresses ever get read, but most candidates will have some evidence that their words have been attended to, if only from the comeback that some of them evoke. A limited number of the undecided or only half decided electors are the ones who form the smattering at public meetings and who do read their election address. These are the ones the marginal seat candidates are·trying to get at and the ones who will finally decide who wins the seat.

After this crucial week-end the candidate goes through the motions of maintaining the momentum of the campaign but by this time the canvassers will be coming back with more definite results. People eventually decide for one of the two major parties in most seats and slowly this becomes apparent. Any candidate in any party has his hardest three days after decision Sunday but the hardest and the longest day of all is polling day.

Touring the polling stations and talking to the tellers takes all day in a rural or even a semi-suburban constituency. It can take the best part of it even in a tight-knit urban area. This in itself is exhausting but it is followed up by the biggest ordeal of all — the count. Tension is again at its highest in the marginal seat. For the candidate who was the MP up to dissolution, the tension is worst of all. I remember the count at Spelthorne in 1966 when Sir Beresford Craddock, the then Conservative holder of the seat, was in some slight danger of losing his seat. Many of his close and long-time colleagues in the House were certainly losing theirs in the heavy Labour poll of that election.

Liberals were losing votes heavily in the direction of the Labour Party and Sir Beresford knew as well as I did that if the pile of Liberal votes on the table in the centre of Staines Town Hall grew too little then he would lose his seat. This was one of the rare occasions when the Conservatives cared that the Liberals should retain their deposit.

The count is a terrifying process. There is a continuous soft rustling sound. The votes are added to the piles in fits and starts and the proportions at any point other than the last fifteen minutes will give no real indication of the final result unless it happens to be a very safe seat. During this particular evening Sir Beresford Craddock sat on the next chair to me with a transistor clapped to his ear: shaking his head as the results from other constituencies came through he was murmuring: 'Ah, poor Pat. Ah, poor Dudley,' as the news of Pat Hornsby Smith's and Dudley Smith's defeat came through.

An indication of the strain and the emotions involved are such that, as I later learned, Dame Pat Hornsby Smith wept as the result was announced. There are certainly plenty of candidates whether they are sacked Members or not who find it hard to conceal their disappointment. Certainly the conviction that one has to dispel to party workers and voters alike about the kind of result one expects do take a bite out of one's own sense of realism. One invariably expects a slightly better result than is achieved.

For the defeated, an even bigger ordeal awaits the outcome of the count. The public, or those supporters who have been allowed into the hall or who have troubled to assemble on the steps of the Town Hall, have to be faced. Even for the winner there is a certain amount of abuse. I remember that the late Wallace Lawler faced a rowdy crowd on the steps of the Birmingham Council House the night of his election in the Ladywood by-election of 1969. But for the defeated, British sportsmanship is in its hour of greatest need: the effort required to summon up a brave smile and a good clean sportsmanlike speech is almost superhuman at times.

For the winner there is a heady moment. The exhilaration of being chosen by the people is as good as the glow of an actor after a well received performance. One MP told me: 'You feel you can do anything.' But can these kaleidoscopic dreams of power turn into reality? When the anti-climax sets in, when the MP finally reaches the House, he surely realises that he has been elected on a party ticket; and party, more his master than the electors, will from that moment dominate his life. The realisation takes time. Most Members reach the House convinced, as John Pardoe says, 'that I could change the world'. If they asked their electors they would learn that this could never be so.

The naïve belief of newer politicians leads them to make earnest promises on the hustings that they can never keep once in the House. The promises of parties are not worth the air they are spent on. Electors know this: but many are still taken in. Older MPs with more experience make promises with tongues in cheek. Time and party politics have made them foxy and cynical. No wonder electors take a dim view of politicians. It is because electoral promises mean nothing that elections are only a very poor apology to democratic principles. Without the means to put promises into action MPs are trapped. There is only one promise a candidate on the hustings has any right to make; to serve and lead. That is a promise any man of integrity can keep even in Parliament.

Unfortunately, if they start out honest, MPs are too often made a little less than idealistic, somewhere along the way. Promises made on the hustings are made without any real knowledge of what Parliament is like.

Parliament is a very different world from that of the hustings: indeed quite different from all aspects of pre-election politics. The Cowboys and Indians clarity of a candidate's appeal to the electorate, of his challenge to his opponents, bears no relation to the complex and subtle shadow box of the politics of Parliament itself.

The candidate attacks the Government or the opposing parties: he accuses his opponents of all manner of neglect and misdemeanour: his efforts are entirely directed to the one aim of getting elected — but once in the House he is awash in his own success. Deprived of its target his militancy — if he has any — looks for new direction.

In this lies a problem. Once inside Parliament the new MP finds that nothing is quite solid. There are no obvious levers to turn, no buttons marked 'instant results' to push. Norman Atkinson describes the experience as 'like being fired out of a gun into a barrel of cotton wool'. Rather like Wilfred Owens' soldier in *Strange Meeting* — 'It seems that out of the battle I escaped into some profound dull tunnel' — new Members are not quite sure at first whether they are dead or alive.

Every new situation requires adjustment and therefore most new Members put their lost feelings down to the fact that they are new boys at the school. As the days pass, however, they are in turn introduced by established Members of their own party to the procedures and facilities of the House. They learn where the bars, restaurants, lavatories, library, smokingroom and offices are. They are sworn in. They meet new colleagues. They experience the thrills of their first State Opening and mostly enjoy their first taste of the heavy traditions of Parliament — whatever they may come to think of them later.

Meanwhile they suffer a disappointment. Parliament for most is not what they expected. Its soporific routine dulls their appetite for attack. They begin to wonder why they came. The surprise is greater for some than for others. To Alisdair Mackenzie, Liberal MP for Ross and Cromarty from 1964 to 1970, it was overwhelming. This middle aged Highland crofter had never before even been to London. Yet he sat in the same Chamber as men and women whose fathers and grandfathers, and in one case at least, whose mother had sat there before them. For them and for those who, like them, have relatives in that other place, the House of Lords, the adjustment would be less strenuous. Familiarity with the climate of Parliament through the medium of a couple of generations of dinner table conversation would at least soften the blow.

Yet familiarity with the House is not a complete defence against the disappointment with Parliament that most new MPs seem to feel. John Gorst is an MP who worked closely with the House of Commons and its personnel for years before his election. In and out of the lobbies and bars with MPs whom he retained as advisers for his public relations business, he absorbed a great deal of the atmosphere of the place. Parliament should have held fewer surprises for him than for many of his contemporaries in 1970. Yet he freely admits: 'If I had realised what Parliamentary life was like I doubt if I would have spent ten years single-mindedly trying to get in.'

Membership of Parliament is about the only job for which there is no formal job description offered to aspirants. Candidates selection committees are more interested in qualities which help candidates to win elections, or such vague concepts as Ministerial ability, or policy leanings than in any ability the candidate may have to deal with the rather misty framework of his Parliamentary job.

From the attitude of most new Members it is clear that they expect to set the world on fire fairly soon after getting elected. It is a common failing of politicians to assume that talk is enough and a few good speeches can solve most problems. In fact the hustings challenger is bound to think of his Parliamentary job in two ways. One, making speeches to astound the House and hypnotise the public, and secondly, to solve constituents' problems at the wave of a taxpayer's form. If great international events have preoccupied the incumbent, he will also, no doubt, have had a vision of himself making a whistle-stop tour of the particular foreign land and returning to report that something will be done. In practice no politician will admit to fantasies as naïve as this. But daydreams of heroic deeds and putting the world to rights like Superman do figure quite prominently in the heads of Parliamentary candidates. The fact is, most of the people who stand for Parliament and spend years of their life trying to get elected are only postponing real political action. They assume that once in Parliament, they will find it easy to solve the sort of problems they come upon during their political campaigning. So they substitute campaigning for direct action. If the drains don't work and if old age pensioners are having a raw deal, if there is something wrong with the educational system, then this is a scandal that will be raised in Parliament once the candidate is elected. At the most this is something which should be dealt with by the sitting MP: once he has said so, the candidate need do nothing himself. No wonder then that he suffers disappointment with Parliament. The people who need to be taken by the scruff of the neck and made to sort out all these injustices are as remote and obscure as before.

There is no easy solution to any political problem. The wiser political animal knows this. The young or new entrant to Parliament may not realise this at first. His grumble will always have been that those who are there are not getting on with the job they have been elected to do. What may be wrong, or what prevents MPs from putting a stop to all the problems of the world at a stroke may never have crossed the minds of the candidates. The same applies to the electors. If as far as they are concerned MPs are a rum lot of promise breakers, does anyone stop to wonder why?

The expectations of new Members as to what the Parliamentary job entails is the main source of their post election blues. Far from finding it is not to their taste, MPs find rather that there is not much for them to do in Parliament.

There is, of course, the routine of Parliament — Question Time Mondays to Thursday at 2.30 p.m.; debates, division, party meetings, committees. But much of the real activity and the involvement in the business of the House through the various committees, through lobbying, raising questions and so on comes later. New Members have to tread carefully before settling into particular habits or attitudes that might be imprudent in terms of future ambitions.

In time these problems are overcome, but there are others. One of the causes of John Gorst's disappointment with Parliament was the nagging discovery that he had more influence on Parliament from the standpoint of a political public relations man than as MP. Gorst's position is unusual, but the cause of his disappointment is pretty universal. Most new MPs are disappointed at their inability to put their politics into practice. The fact that they cannot do so immediately is partly through their unfamiliarity with the methods, such as they are, of getting things done.

But the methods themselves and the atmosphere that pervades the House are thwarting enough to anyone who has been thinking of politics in terms of action.

The Gentleman's Code

One of the dominant conditions that MPs have to adapt themselves to is the gentleman's code. The House has quite rightly been referred to as the best club in the world. Like all clubs it is doubtless a little less good than it used to be. Nevertheless, the club atmosphere prevails.

There are manners and traditions governing behaviour in and between the parties. The gentleman's agreement is the most stifling fact of Parliamentary life. It sometimes defeats the proper use of accepted Parliamentary procedures. Eric Lubbock, as Liberal Whip, was once threatened with a severance of all 'courtesies and facilities' extended between Whips offices. The occasion was one in which he had followed Parliamentary procedures as laid down in Erskine May and sent a letter signed by himself and another Member asking for a writ to be issued for the by-election in Birmingham Ladywood. As Liberal Whip he had every interest in doing so. As Labour Whip, Bob Mellish — who knew the one-time Labour seat would be lost to the Liberals — had every reason for trying to stop the request. In Erskine May it states that if two Members write requesting a by-election to be called, then it must be called. In the end the Ladywood by-election was called: but not before Lubbock had been threatened with the withdrawal of all favours. 'We do not,' said Bob Mellish, referring to the Liberal's ungentlemanly use of accepted procedures, 'do that kind of thing in this House.'

The kind of thing that is done in the House becomes at an early stage the preoccupation of the new Member.

One of the first facets of the code that will be drawn to the attention of a new Member by the established MP that introduces him to the House is that too much publicity is frowned upon. To MPs like Jeffery Archer and John Gorst, used to publicising themselves partly for the sake of their professional interest, this is a severe disadvantage. Publicity is often a measure of power. But as Gorst says: 'To get one's face into the national press more than once or twice can get one a very bad name with one's colleagues.' It can also, he says, 'get one a reputation as a stunt man — like the late Gerald Nabarro for instance'.

Everyone goes in for local publicity in their own constituency. But the fact that national publicity makes one unpopular with other MPs, rules out too enthusiastic an attack on Parliamentary issues by new Members. The need to tread carefully in the first few months is obvious. Enemies are made easily in politics. The best advice a new Member can get is to be told to make himself popular with his own party and at least respected by the others. This can be hard work at times. As Gorst puts it: 'I have my work cut out being agreeable to my colleagues.' Forging popularity is clearly in the interests of any ambitious young Member. The odious odour of ingratiation is therefore quite prevalent at Westminster. Its tranquillising effect on even some of the noisier Members of a new intake are quite well known. Not for nothing does Parliament have a reputation for absorbing dissidents. Many a vocal Parliamentary candidate has been elected in a hail of publicity only to disappear into obscurity within weeks of entering the House.

The first time a Member is likely to break his silence is during the little event known as his maiden speech. This he may make as early as he likes in theory. Bernadette Devlin made hers within half an hour of first arriving at the House. But most Members wait a few weeks until a topic of special interest to themselves or their constituents comes up on the order paper. Some MPs are reputed to wait an uncommonly long time before making their maiden speech and there is the apocryphal story of the Member who was silent for twenty years and then rose to ask the speaker if a window might be opened.

The significance of maiden speeches is not very great and most of them pass unnoticed except in local newspapers. But an ambitious politician can also use his maiden speech to attract the attention of his own party.

Two young Welsh MPs in the 1966 intake of 'bright young' Labour men were waiting to make their verbal debuts on a suitable occasion. When Welsh affairs were due to come up on the order paper one asked the other what he proposed to make the topic of his speech. Having found out he then prepared his own speech on the identical topic with an identical slant to his colleague with the intention of stealing a march on him in the promotion stakes for the Welsh Office. When the moment of the debate came, he had the luck to be called first and managed to leave his colleague so speechless that the other man had to wait for another occasion to make his own maiden speech. (Both men lost their seats in 1974.)

This silly piece of sparring is a good example of the way in which new MPs learn to start building up their personal positions in Parliament. Even MPs who enter the House filled with political zeal can lose their sense of urgency while learning the do's and don'ts of the Parliament club. And playing silly games with the limited opportunities available for gaining distinction is one way of doing this.

If popularity or distinction take time and effort to acquire, active disapproval is relatively easily won. New MPs will be more careful to moderate their activity to avoid stepping out of line with their Parliamentary party. The risk of jeopardising a career is always greatest at its start.

There have been many examples over the years of individual

exclusion: of the virtual sending to Coventry of a Member by a majority of his colleagues. Peter Griffiths, briefly MP for Smethwick and better known as the Parliamentary Leper, was an excluded person for his short period as an MP on account of his delibarete use of racial smears to win the seat in 1964. Enoch Powell was similarly treated by a large number of Members after his own racialist speeches of the late sixties.

These are extreme cases. But the effect on most Members, especially the more impressionable and personally ambitious newcomers is to keep them in the grey area of inoffensiveness, which so often renders them political eunuchs afraid to step out of line. It takes a certain kind of man to brave disapproval. Since one of the innate characteristics of politicians is a desire to be loved, there are not many bold mavericks in Parliament.

Occasionally there is someone who is not afraid to stand apart from the crowd. (One MP once said that if no one would speak to him he would spend his time in the library.) But so often the tragedy of such a man is that he becomes either a clown or an untouchable. Some have survived disapproval to become Ministers in another day. But this is rare. Positions go to the careful. The rash are quickly dispatched into isolation or the back-benches.

The Importance of Being an MP

With all this kind of stricture around it is no wonder new MPs are unhappy. Seldom wonder also that they begin to substitute personal ambition for political, if only on the grounds that the former seem easier to achieve.

Others seriously consider giving up their seats at the next election. Yet so insidious is the charm of Westminster that these curious longings to return to a more honest way of life seem to fade before the five years term is up. By the time the Parliament is dissolved the Members seem to have found sufficient compensation for their disappointments to want to go on being MPs in spite of them. Even John Gorst when I saw him at the Barnet Borough constituency's count after the

February 1974 Election seemed relieved to have been re-elected.

There are compensations of course. MPs are regarded as being important persons; and however bogus this importance is it impresses. No doubt a number of Members are quite convinced of their own importance before they go to the House. Once elected, however, there are numerous tiny ways in which the MP VIP syndrome begins to make itself felt.

Deification is enhanced by appearances on TV. These fall less often to new men than the more established MP pundits, and to some MPs they never happen at all. But then there is radio and the newspapers. Even if only the local media are taking an interest in their regional MPs they will begin to feel important.

In the same way as a teenage beauty blossoming out of schoolgirl gaucherie is made to feel beautiful by the admiration and attention she experiences for the first time, so MPs respond to the increase in their recognition rating by becoming important.

Belief in ones own importance is an essential part of the art of becoming important. MPs are well aware that even if they are not seriously important by virtue of any power or influence they have, they do have some kind of rating so long as they themselves believe in it. That Members do recognise the importance quotient of the letters MP is illustrated by the following example.

In 1971 House of Commons personnel became obliged to carry identification cards due to the security problems during the Irish troubles. A suggestion that this practice should be extended to include MPs brought cries of protest from Fred Peart among others. The very idea that MPs should have to carry passes to get into their own House was too much to bear. However, Peart quietly withdrew his objection when it was discovered that some forty MPs had already been to the Sergeant at Arms to request their passes. As one MP put it: 'You can cash a cheque anywhere with one of these.'

Though John Pardoe says: 'The day I have to carry a pass to get into this House is the day I stop being an MP,' there are apparently a number of Members who have realised that they can get better service by proving to the world that they are Members of Parliament.

In time these minor blessings must woo even the most disenchanted new Member. Only men able to command similar privileges in private life either through money or title would be less likely to succumb to these social advantages. This probably explains why, in spite of disillusion with the political scope available, Members in the end stand for re-election more than willingly. The seductive aspects of Parliamentary life compensate for its problems. In less than one Parliament MPs are beginning to enjoy themselves.

Adapting to Parliament

By this time also, MPs will have decided which aspects of Parliamentary life they like best. Some Members, according to Brian Walden, 'do not like the House'. They spend their time more in the constituencies attending to individual cases. They become the good constituency men; and usually the habitual back-benchers. Others set themselves for Ministerial office and begin working their way into the lower echelons of the promotional hierarchies.

The fact that this can take a long time means that a Member will want to think in terms of staying in Parliament for the rest of his working life. If he is lucky he will have a reasonably safe seat and be able to devote the minimum of time to nursing his constituency. He will also have to pay less attention to local political factors and devote himself more thoroughly to the task of pleasing his party overlords.

By the time the end of his first Parliament comes the MP will have changed considerably. No longer the fresh-faced idealist of the hustings, he will have become in five years flat, a polished politician. By ten years, he will be a fully fledged political fowl. After twenty years an MP is frankly too far gone to be much use to the electors unless he has managed to continue as a faithful constituency man. To any ambitious politician the House is too corrupting a force. Even to the more pedestrian constituency MP there are enough pleasant aspects to the Parliamentary life to enable him to overcome any of the pangs of political conscience of the sort that trouble newer Members.

From the elector's point of view there is a case for limiting the total number of years anyone can spend as an MP to two Parliaments. This way the whole business of representing the electors may come to be regarded more as a service and less as a sinecure.

Meanwhile the causes of new MPs disillusion remain. At the end of every Parliament a few Members leave for reasons which can only be dissatisfaction with the Parliamentary life. Most remain — if their electorate will have them. These are the ones who have managed to adapt themselves to the woolly system of getting things done in Parliament. Or worse have resigned themselves to making the best of the opportunities available for personal gain. For most MPs Parliamentary life is highly addictive. Whether there is power there for the individual Member or not, the trappings of power are much in evidence. Parliament may not have been what most MPs expected but it has something that for most Members makes it worth while staying.

Part Two

RELATIONSHIPS OF POWER

REPRESENTATIVES *v.* EXECUTIVE

Government and the Power of Parliament

Within months of her dramatic win in the 1969 Mid Ulster by-election Bernadette Devlin was saying: 'Parliament does not work.' It was a fashionable view and one shared in and outside the House. There was a feeling that Parliament was a charade, that events taking place there were of no consequence to more real and often violent events outside.

The view that real power lies outside Parliament — in the Executive itself, in Whitehall, with the Trades Unions, the City or at Number Ten, pervades the attitudes of voters both at and between elections. Yet the arguments that Parliament has power if it or its individual Members care to use it has always run counter to this view. Seasoned Members said for instance of Bernadette that she had simply not found the way to make the system work: that she would have done better to bend the ministerial ear in private than hurl abuse across the floor of the House or missiles in the Bogside. Yet many MPs, however they choose to express it, feel that something is wrong.

The first key to the problem, according to John Pardoe, is the relationship of Executive to legislature. 'It is wrong,' he says, 'that one-third of both major parties should be thinking in terms of becoming a part of the Government.' While a further third of the membership of both is living in hope of entering the Government élite at some time, it is impossible to expect Parliament to make representative decisions. 'The Executive,' says Pardoe, himself a fan of the American system, 'should be separated from the legislature.'

Another, now ex-Member, who sees the problem this way is Jeremy Bray. A one-time promising Junior Minister who wrote a book about the workings of Whitehall, Bray sees only too clearly the difficulties of being at one time a Member of the Executive and a part of a Parliament 'whose job it is,' he says, 'to be representative'.

If the representativeness of Parliament conflicts with the pragmatic approach of Government it does so at a time when, according to another ex-MP, Wil Edwards, 'Government is interfering increasingly with every aspect of society'.

'Everything these days,' he says, 'requires Government involvement.' Theoretically, if the Government is composed of MPs who are elected representatives this looks a reasonably acceptable situation. But according to Norman Atkinson 'the influence of the MP is under the circumstances negligible', and he goes on, 'if the Government want to do something there is nothing a Member of Parliament can do to stop them'.

Power for an MP therefore depends upon his becoming a part of the Government. As a part of Government, however, the Member is in a different situation from a back-bencher. The Minister has the power to take decisions whereas the back-bencher is only able to criticise, raise objections, mobilise support. The ordinary MP has a negative role with very few constructive opportunities.

Even Ministers are not omnipotent. It is a characteristic of our political system that power is vested in institutions rather than in the hands of individuals. If there is inflexibility in Government it is partly because of this. Ministers become a part of the institutions. They see political problems in terms of efficient management. Political influences play their part but there is usually one best, cheapest or more productive solution to every problem.

Because of a complex of pressures and often regardless of political considerations and with scant attention to the behest of the party policies, Government makes its decisions in a manner which becomes dangerously detached from the voice of those whose lives will be influenced. As Jeremy Bray says,

'The biggest problem of Government is its detachment from what is going on in the working life of the nation.'

Theoretically, Parliament exists to prevent this isolation. 'MPs,' says Bray, 'are exposed to the whole range of human problems through their constituency work.' Their experience should be translated into the actions of Government. Yet somehow this happens less through the formal channels of legislation than through the backroom pressures and the personal influence of those with bargains to drive.

One of the troubles of the system is that Parliament as a whole finds it impossible to prevent the passage of Government legislation — primarily because of the whipping system and the formal division of the House into Government and Opposition. The crucial factor in preserving the power and isolation of the Executive is the Government's ability to command a majority in Parliament. Usually, the Governing party can pull in most of its own Members on any matter of importance to its survival, and usually also a working majority is considered to be a sign of health and stability in the system.

Unfortunately it has become more of an excuse in recent years for the concentration of power, presidentially almost — at Number Ten Downing Street, where there is even a special policy unit attached now. Even the collegiate nature of the Cabinet, considered an essential aspect of the so-called Westminster system of Government, has slowly eroded away into a kind of pecking order with the Prime Minister at the top. Concurrent with this trend, Parliament has not only decreased in potency, but has also failed increasingly in its traditional function as a buffer between the acts of a remote Executive and the reaction of people on the receiving end.

The erosion of some of the fundamentals of our two-party democratic system — the collegiate cabinet and the safety valve Parliament has brought with it cries for a change of a different kind. If Government and Parliament were too constrained by the system to respond to the mixed pressures of a more rapidly changing society, then a system presenting the opportunity for a greater flexibility, for a greater variety of political expression seemed necessary. Jo Grimmond, expressing concern that the system could be changing less quickly than society and responding too slowly to the expectations of an increasingly educated electorate, said in 1972* 'The relationship between Government, parties and Parliament is changing, as the whole nineteenth-century system is changing and needs bringing up to date.' He went on, 'I hope it will change rapidly enough but there is a real danger that it will be left a long way behind.'

The system itself was to demonstrate a curiously conscious desire for change. During 1972 and 1973 the electorate with that rather psychic collective wisdom began to elect Liberals and Scottish Nationalists in by-elections. Throughout 1973 disillusion with Government by either of the established entities of the two largest parties became the focus of political expression. The strange rise of the Liberals, on a tidal wave of escalating opinion poll scores, drew forth calls for a balance of power situation, for coalitions, for unity and the middle way. If some of this was gross in its lack of understanding of the nature of democracy it was still an expression of the feeling common to most individuals in Parliament and outside, that the system was becoming more and more a caricature of its textbook self. The desired change manifested itself almost exactly as the collective mind had wished. The numbers were not quite perfect, nor was the balance of power held by the Liberals alone. But for the first time, the two-party system of elections had produced a multi-party hotch-potch in Parliament.

Whereas the politicians of the two leading parties had consistently called for strong government, for a clear mandate, had demanded to know who ruled Britain, the voters had managed to produce the reverse — and something I called for myself — a strong Parliament: at least in theory. As David Howells, a prominent Minister in the previous Conservative administration, wrote in an article to *The Times* on March 26th, 1974, 'Like it or not, the rules of the game have for the time being been changed radically in Parliament's favour. Crude power now rests again in the Commons to frustrate Executive deci-

* *Guardian* feature.

sions, almost any evening of the week and to present a constant threat to the Government's existence.'

But the results were still not very constructive. As David Steel, Liberal Chief Whip, said at the time: 'The results if anything are more negative than positive. The Government has had to take some things out of its programme as laid down in the Queen's speech. It has had to tone down its proposals.' If the situation had changed at all, he said, it was that now 'votes could be taken, some of which could go against the Government, forcing it to reconsider its position rather than to resign.'

In time this may be an important constitutional precedent; one which could operate to effectively maintain the power of Parliament in the face of a strong Whip even where the administration had a clear majority. The idea that Parliament could, in a rogue vote, put the Government down and force a General Election was itself quoshed by the Prime Minister Harold Wilson when in the debate following the Queen's speech on March 12th, 1974, he said: 'The Government intends to treat with respect, but not with exaggerated respect, the results of any snap vote or any snap division. The Government,' he stated, 'would reconsider its position and make a definitive statement ... but the Government would not be forced to go to the country except in a situation in which every Hon. Member in the House was voting, knowing the full consequences of his vote.' A vote of confidence and not a snap vote where the Government would be caught with its pants down in the absence of a three-line Whip, would be the only way to discover whether the Government was really required to resign. So in a sense the onus was still on MPs to knuckle down in the interests of the nation and keep the Government in power. Their collective power as a Parliament therefore was still constrained by the formality of the politics of Parliament.

The Executive is still in control of the initiative — still in charge of the creative aspects of policy formation. It is, on the admission of one ex-Parliamentary candidate, easier to get Legislation on to the Statute Book from outside Parliament than from within. (He himself, as expert in a particular field, influenced the Number Ten think tank to the extent of having a Bill put through the Parliament of which he had himself failed to become a Member.)

The only difference between the power of the Executive in a minority situation and that of a strongly backed Government is that the legislation initiated will have more consensus qualities, will offend fewer blocks of opinion.

But if Parliament lacks collective power, are MPs really the useless eunuchs they appear to be? Jeremy Bray offers a ray of hope in saying that 'Parliament still offers a scene in which it is possible to operate effectively'. There are, in fact, ways and means of achieving political ends as a Member of Parliament. Bernadette Devlin herself acknowledged this in a TV interview with Robert Key. When asked by Key why it was she remained an MP if she thought Parliament did not work, Bernadette replied: 'I am listened to. You would not be sitting here asking me questions if I was just plain Bernadette Devlin. You are talking to me because I am Bernadette Devlin, MP.'

The same applies to all other Members who are unhappy with Parliament. The fact that an individual is an MP gives him an opportunity to be listened to. Whatever else it does or does not do, the title MP is in itself a wrench to open doors which would otherwise remain closed. It is this power which MPs apply in the various aspects of their work.

The opportunity to be listened to is the one that ordinary citizens lack. Anyone may stand up at Hyde Park Corner and exercise the traditional freedom of speech, but he will not set the world on fire. The simple fact that the media select and carry the messages which make news, relegates all those who have no real claim to fame to a position of no influence. Real influence comes through being called upon to comment on national and international events, and this influence is in some way a power over the minds of those listening. When Enoch Powell made his speeches against coloured immigrants, each one was followed by a rise in the number of 'Paki bashing' incidents in Wolverhampton. When Denis Healey spoke out against the South African régime following his visit there in 1971 he moved world opinion against South Africa. On a lighter level Miss Joan Lestor complained in the House about kerb crawlers: and another MP referred to London's Northern line as a cattle truck with the result that the press called it the misery line in subsequent reports for weeks afterwards.

None of these incidents can be proved to have lasting effect. Seldom do they result in changes in the law. But they are part of the pressure which MPs may use on behalf of the electors to voice displeasure about the way things are going. Right or wrong, MPs can this way represent for public consumption the moods and wishes of minorities. They can bring local, domestic, national or international events to the notice of a wider audience than any other commentator upon the scene.

To be listened to is, however, not alone enough to justify the fact of being a Member of Parliament. What powers do Members of Parliament have over the institutions that run Britain: what power do they have against the might of Government? If they have any power at all is that merely stopping power or is there an opportunity to initiate reforms?

Power at the Grass Roots

The real power of MPs is best illustrated by their effectiveness in achieving solutions to constituents' problems.

The primary relationship of politics in Britain is that between constituent and MP. This relationship is more intimate and responsible in the single Member constituency system that we have in Britain than in the multi-Member constituencies of some Common Market countries. The basic job of every MP is to see that his constituents get a square deal and the most direct way of doing this is to solve their problems individually.

Representing the electors *en masse* is by no means simple. It is impossible to represent all constituents politically. No political posture yet devised is quite all things to all men. Yet Andrew Bowden is able to say: 'I represent all my constituents all the time whoever they voted for.' In other words the MP stands between his constituents and all forms of erosion of their rights whether by Government, by bureaucracy, by the Law or by other human beings. He is in effect an ombudsman; the man who stands between people and State. Under such a system a Conservative Member may help a striker to gain national assistance and a Labour man may help a rich constituent to recover thousands of pounds from the Inland Revenue.

The success rate of MPs on this sort of level is very high. As a result most Members of Parliament regard constituency case work as the most rewarding aspect of the Parliamentary career. This applies particularly to MPs who are settled into the role of perpetual back-bencher; the man who is more of a true MP than his colleagues who still have their eyes on the front bench.

Perhaps the most astonishing aspect of the MP as constituency ombudsman is the ease with which he sorts out problems that have previously been insoluble to the citizen concerned. Gas Boards, telephone engineers, housing managers and social security officers swing into action at the sound of the local MP's name. A telephone call by the Member of Parliament to the Town Hall is the key to every bureaucratic muddle in which the constituent is likely to find himself.

Yet there is no real reason why this should be so. It is the fact that Members of Parliament are assumed to be powerful which gives them the authority to get things done. The illusion of power is, in fact, the reality of power at the constituency level.

John Gorst says that 'any fool with MP after his name can make local officials jump'. This to him is not the stuff of politics. He is only partly right. Constituency case work is the fundamental activity of the representative system; and representation means dealing with the consequences of Government action. Since Government action is extending further into every aspect of the nation's life, the constituency function of the MP is increasingly valuable. Ignorance of the ways in which new legislation affects individuals is one factor which increases the constituent's dependence on MPs specialist understanding of Parliamentary goings on. Not that the electorate have ever been particularly well informed on matters affecting their interest. However, the pretence at informing voters, which goes on both during elections and the Parliamentary term, has whetted their appetite for a more accurate flow of data.

The Common Market Entry fracas was just one case in point. The most unfortunate aspect of that, however, was the way in which it highlighted the fact that the ignorance of the electorate is only marginally darker than that of the MPs. Marcus Lipton told me that this problem applies in all areas, 'I often have to go and find out what the Law is on a certain subject before I can do anything to solve a problem.'

However ignorant the Member is, it happens to be his job to find out and understand the best way to act on his constituents' behalf when faced with the complexities of modern bureaucracy. Marcus Lipton is one who spends most of his time on constituents' cases. Well known as a kind of people's friend, Lipton says: 'People are not interested in the march of technology.' He also says ordinary people have contracted out because as he says 'the modern Welfare State is too demanding and too complex for people to cope with'.

Horizons have widened — the global village is an uncomfortable fact. Catapulted in three generations from the serene world of community life, local gossip, hearsay, horses and carts, and in many cases gaslight, people now in their sixties and seventies are struggling to grasp floods of international implications. World-shrinking devices like television have even forced out the parochial element in many newspapers and magazines. Instead of the odd bit of tittle-tattle about the local squire, we are now treated to high-pitched international gossip about Jackie and Ari, the White House, the Burtons, heart transplants, the sex life of Giant Pandas, and pollution of the Great Lakes. Apart from all this there are multi-megaton bombs, metrication, and push-button war to be grasped. No wonder methods of escapism like drugs or dropping out are becoming so popular and not only with the hippie fringe. It certainly is no surprise that the ordinary citizen would rather have his electricity bill put right than hear about the technological spin off from Concord; have his rates reduced rather than upset himself about the poisoning of the oceans; or have a shilling off beef than worry about economic sanctions against South Africa. Rightly or wrongly, people are genuinely confused by the flow of events over which they have no control whatsoever. More than ever, then, it is the duty of the Member of Parliament to help them.

Not all the problems constituents will bring to MPs can be solved. One Member complains that: 'People come to one because they have a vague feeling that something is wrong with their marriage or their life. Not because they have any definite problem.' Members of Parliament come into the same category as doctors and priests; the open door is an invitation to the lonely and the defeated, the sick, the tired and the unhappy. It is just as well that they have somewhere to go. Even if the MP feels that there is nothing he can do for them, he has exercised the responsibility of his position by listening.

At the same time a number of genuine problems will go unnoticed by the Member. Unless people bring their difficulties to their MP he is unlikely to find out about them. The range of problems covered and the number dealt with will vary from Member to Member. The better the reputation of the Member for constituency work the more letters and problems he will receive. Marcus Lipton, for instance, deals with about thirty cases a week, each at a different state of progress. He holds a surgery every week. Problems covered will include a fair sprinkling of tax, planning, social security and housing difficulties. Often he says he has to find out from scratch how to tackle the problem, who are the officers. 'Bureaucracy,' he says, 'is not only getting worse. It changes its cogs more often. I used to know all the officers in the local ministries, but now they keep changing. I never get to know them.' Then the Ministries themselves keep changing form. 'I have to write to Edinburgh,' says Lipton, 'because someone from Brixton has been done out of a few shillings tax.'

Marcus Lipton spends 90 per cent of his time on constituency problems, i.e. individual case work. He regards this as essential to the whole business of Parliament. 'I am in touch with people and people are what politics is all about,' he says. 'The tensions which arise and the injustices are what one learns about through casework. It is the object of wise legislation to smooth these out.' Clearly the grass roots are the source of all political change. The closer Members of Parliament get to them the more accurate will their definition be of the needs and moods of ordinary life. Once a Minister, however, his timetable alone isolates the MP from grass roots reality.

Representing the Constituents in the House

If the Member of Parliament has a high level of success in dealing with local authority and Ministry officials he is some of the time handling problems which should be dealt with by local councillors. This is to some extent a comment on the workings of local Government and the Member will in any case refer the solution of the problem to the local official concerned. Having acted as a higher authority and arbiter in his own constituency the Member is in a rather different position when it comes to putting his constituents' problems to the House, or rather the Executive.

The main occasion on which constituency questions are raised officially at Parliament is during Question Time. This occurs at 2.30 p.m. every afternoon except Friday during a normal Parliamentary week. The questions raised will concern broad constituency matters rather than individual concerns on the whole.

It is a matter of real doubt as to whether asking questions in the House has any real value other than publicity. The whole performance of Question Time is a mixture of cynical behaviour from both Members and Ministers alike. The former are out to get themselves on the record either with their local party or their floating voters. Often enough they trot out questions to which they well know the answers simply in order to get into the press.

But it is the activities of Ministers which are most seriously in danger of making Question Time a farce. In theory this is the period of time when the Prime Minister and his Ministerial colleagues account to the House and — through the media — to the nation at large. If one of the slender pivots of the British Parliamentary system is ministerial accountability, then recent revelations about question rigging in the House are more than serious.

In November 1971 there was a row about question rigging. The Ministry of the Environment's four Ministers had been handing prepared questions to Conservative back-benchers with the purpose of blocking any awkward ones from the Opposition. If the time allotted to the Environment Ministry was thus taken up with their own questions, clearly the processes of democracy, however feeble, were being thwarted utterly.

It emerged that the question rigging had been arranged to thwart similarly planted questions from the Opposition. The Labour Whips, it was claimed in defence, had also been misappropriating Question Time by planting streams of awkward questions to the Environment Ministers. When interviewed by an inquiry into the affair, one Minister told the inquiry that he had indulged in this defence mechanism before, and Julian Amery, then Housing Minister, said that he thought there was nothing abnormal in the practice.

A more serious aspect of this particular case was the extent to which civil servants' time had been used in concocting answers to 'plant' questions. Any question which a Minister proposes to answer either orally or in written form requires research for the answer. This reason is usually reckoned to cost the taxpayer about £10 to £15 for civil servants' time. If the question is to be answered orally then the Member whose question it is will be entitled to ask one supplementary question. Since Ministers are not mind-readers they can assume at best that the supplementary will be one of several alternatives. All the alternatives need to have answers prepared for them. This, in turn, takes up further civil service time at further cost to the taxpayer.

Mr. Arthur Lewis, MP for West Ham, is a prolific question asker. Referred to by sarcastic Ministers as 'the last of the great askers', Mr. Lewis was held to have been responsible for costing the nation £13,296 in the first half of the 1970–74 Parliament. At the last count he was alleged to have asked 2,222 questions in one session alone. All his own work! At least the civil service would only have to research the answers. In the case of Ministerial question rigging it turned out that civil servants were being put to work to prepare the questions as well.

No wonder the cost of Question Time over any one session was last given as £400,000.

The practice of planting questions is fairly habitual. As Peter Kirk says: 'Of course, we all do that — rigging questions, I mean, but for written not oral answer!'* Agreeing that the Ministry of the Environment had gone too far, Kirk went on to say, 'Question Time is rapidly becoming a farce.' By way of example he said, 'People ask the same question every time our turn comes round.' Kirk, when Under-Secretary for the Royal Navy, says he was asked the same question on the Beira patrol three times running. 'The answer,' he says, 'was the same every time. It had to be. That was the official answer.' The question was only being asked, he said, for the sake of the interests the Member represented.† 'Most MPs,' he said, 'are not actively trying to seek the answer.' They are in fact putting themselves on the record. Most of the serious questions are asked in written form and answered that way too. Though, of course, even that process can be misused.

Question Time nevertheless has to be maintained. For all its farcical abuse it is the public arena in which Ministerial accountability is put through the hoop. The phrase 'I should find it difficult to defend in Parliament' is a traditional Ministerial quote. Jeremy Bray reminded me that it still applies. The Commons can make an uncommon fuss at times and Ministers are very susceptible to bad publicity. On such small safety valves does our constitution stand.

Not all the questions raised during Question Time are about specific local constituency interests. Many if not most will be about national or even international matters. Some will be about extraordinary trivia like dog licences and others about deeply important Government activities. The greatest effect of any question is the influence it might achieve on public opinion, if it should happen to be well enough publicised to

* Report on Arthur Lewis — see *The Guardian* 10.8.1972. 'I only arsked', by Dennis Barker.

† Full report of Commons Question Rigging by Ministry of Environment Report by Commons Select Committee on Question Time in Parliament.

create follow-ups and even start some kind of public debate in the media. Unfortunately for our political system, dog licences are more likely to do this than any serious attack on Government competence in important areas of our national life.

The Power of the Chamber

Like Question Time Parliamentary debates are good sources of publicity to party or individual Member. Unlike Question Time, debates are a part of the legislative process. They are also that part of the Parliamentary process which the public most associates with its concept of Parliamentary life. It is the debates which are reported most of all the parts of the legislative process. As far as the public is concerned there might be no other stages in the production of a Parliamentary Act. If MPs appear to be a useless lot of clowns it is partly because of the publicity given to the events in the Chamber and in the voting lobbies.

Yet the public aspect of Parliament is essential to democracy. The Chamber is an arena. But in many ways it is a pointless one. The traditional function of debate is to influence the minds of those who will decide an issue, before they vote. The recurrence of three-line Whips makes any House of Commons debate a farce in that sense. When two-line or single-line Whips are operating, the attendance of Members is slight. Members have too much to do to be able to sit in the Chamber solidly from 2.30 p.m. until 10.00 p.m. or later listening to debates, unless ordered to do so by the Whips. The connection between debate and vote is therefore broken.

The function of debates in the Chamber is mainly that of providing a public spectacle of democracy in practice. People can come to the House — if they can get in — and sit in the public gallery. They can even sit in on Committees. Alternatively, they can read the newspapers, listen to the radio, watch television, or if they are really keen, read *Hansard* every week. The value of having a public debate should not however, be underestimated. Every Bill that goes through Parliament comes three times to the Chamber of the House, and the snags and pitfalls, pros and cons are aired there and reported in the press. Any Member of Parliament who thinks something is wrong can say so publicly in the logical context of debate. This is one way in which Members can influence, if not the shape of legislation, at least its public reception. The debate gives the public the opportunity to hear arguments for and against a piece of legislation, rather than simply providing them with the final solution. Otherwise it has little positive impact.

Short of riot and bloodshed, and sometimes it seems (viz. Ulster) not even then, the Government proceeds along its path. The opinions of MPs make not the slightest impression on the Government under the normal circumstances, and the concerted forces of the Opposition, though howling for blood, can wash out not a line of what the Ministerial finger writes. Only rebellion in the Governing party, by endangering the Parliamentary majority, shakes the Executive bulldozer from its path.

The Chamber is probably the weakest point of influence available to back-benchers. Frequently it is simply a safety valve for pent-up feelings. It is the point at which the division between the two sides of the House seems at its deepest and most artificial. At times that division flares to hatred, and hard words are hurled about the Chamber. Worse, there have been cases of physical assault many times since the days of Oliver Cromwell, and several times within living memory.

One occasion was when Miss Bernadette Devlin, incensed that the Speaker would not call her in the furore which followed the shooting of thirteen civilians in Londonderry, hurled herself at the Home Secretary, pulled his hair and scratched his face. Her anger was lasting. 'I'm only sorry,' she growled later in a television interview, 'that I didn't get him by the throat.' She was not the first woman to act violently in the Chamber. The late Bessie Braddock preceded her by crossing the floor to a Tory Member whom she took by the tie and threatened: 'I'll punch you in the face.' Amongst the other fisticuffs were those of Emanuel Shinwell, who also remembers when Leo Amery crossed the floor and slapped a Labour

Member across the face. A typical incident was the one in which Jeremy Thorpe was jostled and pushed around by James Hamilton and other Labour MPs; and for nothing less than sticking to his principles on the Common Market. No doubt, in times past men drew their swords at the tactical insults of debate, where now they merely throw a punch or two.

Lighter-hearted diversions have taken place. Bessie Braddock once danced a jig in the middle of the floor. Dame Irene Ward was removed for refusing to stop speaking. Frivolities are part of the repartee of the Chamber as much as brutalities. The public tends to disapprove of these extremities of behaviour, expecting more serious things from their representatives. The fact that the talking shop of the Chamber has no obvious effect on the legislation is what makes electors distrustful of their 'schoolboy capers'. But perhaps this is also what drives MPs to buffoonery and violence alike. Any schoolteacher knows that frustration makes the pupils both frivolous and aggressive.

The frustration of the Chamber is that is achieves nothing positive in political terms. It is responsible for much of the talk about Parliament not working. Yet some Members are happier in the Chamber than in any other political situation; but Members who make the most headlines and the most Parliamentary noise are not always the most respected of their colleagues. As Brian Walden says: 'People outside never see what really counts — who are the buffoons; who, the really able people.' What really counts is not what goes on in the Chamber but what happens behind the scenes. Influence is most effective when it is most private. Peter Kirk says: 'The way to get things done is to tackle a Minister privately and get him when policy is still being formulated.' Better still, nobble the Ministers' advisers. One need not be an MP to lobby a Minister, but he is more likely to listen to a Member of Parliament, and preferably one from his own party.

Bent Ears and Cross-Benchers

There is no evidence that talking to a Minister actually helps to get reforms on to the Statute Book. The most a Member can hope for is to be consulted as a specialist during the constructive phases of policy formation; otherwise he is inevitably in the negative position of trying to get something deleted or amended. There is little hope that any Minister will listen to some idea that is totally contrary to his own intentions. Lobbying is only successful when minds are on the same track in the first place.

Like thinking does occur across party barriers. The thought that a Left Winger from the Tribune Group would be able to talk a diehard Conservative Minister into nationalising an industry is hardly credible; but stranger things have happened. It was the Conservatives who nationalised Rolls-Royce with the support of most of the Labour Party; and it was the Left Wing intellectual, Tony Wedgwood Benn, who as Minister of Technology gave twenty millions to the collapsing Upper Clyde Shipbuilders in 1969. If back-benchers do have any success in bending the ear of a Minister it is probably for non-ideological favours; major road improvements in the Member's constituency are carried out with Government aid; local industry can be helped to expand with Government money. Again, these are favours more likely to fall to Government rather than the Opposition back-benchers. Cross-party liaison between front-benchers and between back-benchers of both parties is more frequent than is imagined. Liberals and Independents join in with this too when their support is needed or when they in turn have something on.

Although it is the divisions between parties which when publicised reap the most scorn, it is the cross-dealing which can be the most dangerous. This is the dreaded consensus which became the favourite journalistic term during the late sixties. Following the intensified party division which had occurred during the early period of the Wilson Government, a sudden desire to agree was a natural reaction.

The public had become weary of the inter-party bickering which had preoccupied the media and there was talk of pulling together, backing Britain, businessmen's governments and all manner of undemocratic nonsense. The Liberal Party under

Jeremy Thorpe also fell for consensus and it was virtually impossible to get anyone to criticise the Government. The dangers inherent in this front bench and CBI TUC collusion over every major issue soon began to show. Back-benchers of all parties became visibly embittered. At every political level outside Government there was a breaking away to extremes which produced the racialist ravings of Enoch Powell on the one hand, and the fashionable banalities of Tariq Ali and his Left Wing Euro-demonstrators on the other. Formal opposition was at an all-time low. True opposition therefore had to come from outside. The stock of Parliament fell as its impotence against the might of the establishment consensus reached dangerous proportions.

Not all inter-party cross fertilisation alienates minorities; but in a two-party system it is bound to do so if it emerges from behind the scenes as it did so on this occasion in the form of '*faits accomplis*' above even the MPs' heads. The formal division of interests is a healthy public posture. Meanwhile behind the scenes MPs collaborate across party barriers to sponsor Bills and support each other in Parliamentary organisations and committees. There are inter-party groups formed to press for legislation and reforms of the procedures of the House. Members will support each other verbally in debate where treasured political values are not at stake. In fact the sweet talk in *Hansard* between 'dear and respected friends', on opposite sides of the House, is not hard to believe. There is, in fact, a camaraderie. Members, with individual exceptions, like Enoch Powell and Andrew Faulds or Harold Wilson and Ted Heath, do not go around hating each other.

There is an overlap of views between Members. Only the extremes in any party find it impossible to meet with the other party on the majority of issues. Members in opposing parties sometimes have more in common with each other than with some Members of their own Party. One Conservative Member told me that he had 'much more in common with certain Labour Members than with the 1922 Committee men'.

On the other hand, Members do have a tendency to keep with their own friends and these are not often Members of other parties. Certain groups have their own hunting grounds. On the whole the Strangers Bar and the tea-room are the principle haunts of the Trades Union Members; the Harcourt Room or Restaurant more favoured by older Conservatives and the smoother Labour men.

Power in Committees

However the informal movements and acquaintances of MPs influence the course of legislation it is in the formal committees that cross-party relationships make their official mark. There are two principle sorts of Committee of the House; Select Committees and Standing Committees. The former are not directly related to legislation and have no proportionate representation of parties in their composition. Standing Committees are an integral part of legislative procedure and are made up of Members of the parties in approximate proportion to the representation in the House. The Governing party always has a majority on these committees: but even then there is ample opportunity for difficulties between party positions to be ironed out. Under a minority Government, committees take on a new power.

The Standing Committee stage occurs after the Second Reading of the Bill. By this time the Bill has taken shape and there is not much an Opposition MP on a committee can do to alter its total structure except in the detail. Opposition Members on a committee for a Bill which the Opposition opposes can only try to amend the Bill: but Government Members may want to amend it also. The composition of the committee and the sympathies between the various Members on it have a profound effect on this stage of the Bill. Hard line party attitudes are usually abandoned and there is consensus. As to whether this is a bad thing Brian Walden says: 'Committees do lead to consensus but this serves to balance the artificial effect the division of the Chamber has on the legislation.'

The Committee stage more than any other is the one which helps to remove the anomalies in legislation. The Members on the Standing Committee are there to think of examples among their own constituents who might suffer or benefit unduly from clauses in the Bill.

'Yet in spite of the hours spent, debating in the Chamber and talking in Committee,' says Norman Atkinson, 'contradictions go through.' Legislation, tempered even by MPs personal experience of constituents problems with, what Marcus Lipton calls 'the growing tangle of bureaucracy', still results in odd cases of injustice or hardship here and there. Sometimes this is just bad drafting, and at others a total lack of foresight on the part of the legislators. Sometimes the legislation is badly conceived and at others, perhaps, subject to too much influence from some MPs or from vested interests on one side or the other.

If Standing Committees are consensus prone, then Select Committees are likely to be more so. In the first place they tend to be made up of specialists. There are many highly qualified people in the House. Specialists often find that their common experience helps them to agree with each other: and party differences are even less important on Select Committees than on Standing Committees.

Because the Select Committee is an investigatory Committee, it calls upon other Members of Parliament and outside personnel to give evidence. It may be investigating aspects of Government or Ministerial activity, various facets of the work of the House, codes of practice, and so on. The number of Select Committees is increasing. In 1961 there were seventeen Select Committees sitting and in 1971 there were twenty-three. Civil servants can be called to give evidence to a Select Committee and Peter Kirk says: 'This is very welcome. The trend towards Select Committees is a very good thing if it means that civil servants can be made accountable.' Since civil servants have considerable influence over Ministers this is logical and valuable — in spite of the fact that, as Kirk adds: 'They don't like it of course.'

The actual effect of the Select Committee on Government is dubious. There is a tendency for Select Committees to be set up on the same principle as Royal Commissions. They are convened in response to some demand; they sit, report and then silence; the heat goes out of the issue and the press lose interest. As David Howell wrote in *The Times* (26.3.74): 'In the last analysis the reality has been inescapable. Power is elsewhere. The Government can ignore or damn with faint praise, the work of Select Committees. Departments can withhold at will information about the way policy is being made. And the Whips and party managers can safely give them low priority.'

The minority Government situation after February 1974 brought fresh hopes to the supporters of Committee work. David Howell writing in the same *Times* article said: 'With no party apparatus in control the Select Committees could develop a momentum of their own. Their demands for more information into what is going on in Government and the Civil Service could be put forward with new authority. In the past,' went on Mr. Howell, 'attempts to update and open out the processes of central government, the weak link has been Parliament itself.' The development of new departments, agencies and the improvement of the management structure of Whitehall had not been paralleled by an improvement in Parliament's ability to make them accountable. 'If the new bodies,' wrote Howell, 'were to be genuinely more accountable to Parliament and the public for their operation, then Parliament for its part had to be able to cope. There needed to be informed, well focused and lively Parliamentary committees before which each agency or unit could be regularly and intelligently held to account.'

An increase in Select Committees would be welcomed by many Members on the grounds that it gives back-benchers an opportunity to take a constructive interest in the powers of Government. There is also the pertinent argument that committees encourage Members to specialise, to use their own expertise instead of blundering around in a generalised quagmire of ignorance: the pro-committee MPs claim that much of the debating time in the Chamber is given over to uninformed comment. Increased standing committee work and a reduction of the general debating time allotted to the process of legislation would, these Members claim, enable MPs to become more specialised and therefore more influential in a restricted sphere.

The traditionalists, however, counter with the opinion that too much specialisation is dangerous, that the open forum of the Chamber is essential to the survival of democracy and that committees give too much opportunity for experts to push things through by sleight of hand. Enoch Powell once remarked that 'anything which curtails true debate on the floor of the House diminishes the power of Parliament'. The questions asked by MPs were not meant to be based on the expert point of view but, 'the question that any ordinary member of the public can ask should be asked by MPs'.

One attraction of Parliament as it stands at present is that it gives scope to the Member to exert his influence over a variety of ever-changing issues. When a Member sits on a Select Committee in the morning he can still interest himself in a range of other subjects during the afternoon and evening. But there is still not much a Member can do to further a particular reforming idea. Committee work is a thing of nudges and winks, a slow process of subtle manoeuvring. No wonder Jo Grimmond exclaims his horror at the thought of 'Government by Committee'.

Initiating Legislation

The only area of Parliamentary activity which does offer a Member the opportunity for some form of self-gratification is that of Private Members Bill. An MP can introduce a Bill in two ways: under the Ten Minute Rule, or through the ballot for Private Members Bills which takes place once a year. This may sound like plenty of opportunity, but in practice the odds of getting a Bill through are something like that of a fox getting away from the hounds on a bad day for foxes.

The ballot for Private Members Bills is the most significant occasion, but the most difficult of all. As David Steel says, 'the ballot is in fact a raffle'. 'The Members put their names on to pieces of paper and put them in a hat. Then someone, the Speaker, pulls them out.' The first half-dozen or so names are the only ones out of the 400 odd hopefuls to be given an opportunity to sponsor a Bill. Members put their names in without any clear ideas of what their Bill will be about. If they are lucky enough to draw, as David Steel was, they will probably be approached by an outside pressure group. Steel got a Bill through on Abortion Law Reform. He was lucky: most Private Members Bills die at birth. But if Labour Government was good for one thing, it was good for Private Member sponsored legislation. Homosexual law reform, abolition of the death penalty, abortion law reform and divorce reform were four long pressed for pieces of reforming legislation which got through with the support of most Labour MPs, Liberals, Independents and some Conservatives.

If a Bill gets past the first few hurdles it can still be killed by a shortage of Parliamentary time. Most Parliamentary sessions run through twelve months with a new one beginning every autumn. In 1966–67, however, the Parliamentary session ran for fifteen months, so that the Government could complete important Bills of its own. Usually, any Bill uncompleted is killed at the end of the session and has to go back to the beginning of the snakes and ladders board. Steel's abortion Bill would, he says, 'never have got through had it not been for the long session'.

The Ten Minute Rule produces far more attempts at Private Members legislation than the ballot. One such Bill was the late Gerald Nabarro's controversial Bill on cigarette advertising. This Bill depended for its survival on Government support, although it had sponsors from all parties among the nine names putting it forward with Sir Gerald. Had the Government put a Whip out against the Bill, it would not have survived. The initial Government reaction was to oppose the Bill which was too anti-smoking for the tobacco lobby in Parliament to suffer. Among other clauses was one which would prohibit smoking in public places. When this was amended out, the Bill got Government support and there is now legislation which enforces the carrying of printed health warnings upon all packets of cigarettes and cigarette advertisements.

Such are the nuts and bolts of Private Members legislation: big sweeping reforms intending to come from the ballot winners, cog and loophole stuff from the Ten Minute Rule. Even so the amount of time allotted to this type of legislation is derisory. The Ten Minute Rule operates every week on two afternoons and competition is stiff. Most lose out in their second reading which always takes place on Fridays. Friday, being a day when most Members with far-distant constituencies skip their attendance at Westminster, this is obviously something of a handicap to Private Members Bills.

Most MPs are agreed that there should be more time for Private Members Bills. But where is the time to come from? Already the Parliamentary terms are eroding the vacations and the pressure of legislation is increasing. Not only is there Government-sponsored legislation but there are the increasing number of Private Bills going through the House. These are related to independent authorities, like London Transport whose terms of operation still have to be approved by Parliament. These Bills are by no means easily passed. As the young man in the Committees office of the House remarked to me: 'The Mersey Docks and Harbours Bill was one of those and there was one hell of a kerfuffle over that.'

The Power of Information

Most Parliamentary time goes to Government-sponsored Bills and to Private Bills. But shortage of time is not the only disadvantage this form of legislation faces. Brian Walden says: 'One of the most severe disadvantages faced by Members introducing Bills is the lack of specialist advice.' Walden himself introduced a Bill to protect privacy. He was fortunate in having the support of the National Council of Civil Liberties as a source of research and information. But such an organisation can hardly compete with the vast machinery of the civil service which a Government has to call upon for its own legislation. The best a back-bencher can hope for when introducing legislation is to get the kind of support which David Steel received from the Society for Abortion Law Reform. If a Member wants to make a contribution to any legislation he has to be informed.

One of the dangers of MPs' lack of ready information is that they can be prey to sophisticated lobbyists. Industrial experts purveying specialist information in a readily assimilable form can give individual opposition MPs a stick with which to clobber the Government. I have it on authority from such an industrial source that a number of interests are very successful in getting Members to take up their speeches. That this is to some effect is illustrated by the fact that amendments/ legislation have been helped through the House by similar practises. (There are other ways in which MPs can help the aims of lobbyists. These are discussed more fully in Part 3, Chapter 2.)

Often the ignorance of Members is not due to a lack of available information; it can be the result of a failure to read the material provided. Marcus Lipton showed me a pile six inches deep of Government White Papers and Bills. 'The term only began last week,' he said, 'and I'm supposed to read all this lot. It's only next week's business. How the hell are we supposed to cope?' How indeed?

Specialisation of interests is one answer. Alternatively, help from a good research assistant can cut through the scrub of inessential detail. But there is no substitute for a Member's own expertise in a subject and apart from direct experience in a field this can only be acquired by reading. Claims that outside professional interests can increase a Member's direct experience are mostly countered by the view that they take up more time than they are worth as sources of unbiased knowledge.

Other aids to knowledge come from such specialist Parliamentary groups as that on Science and Technology jointly made up of scientifically interested MPs and a number of eminent scientists. Likewise association with outside political pressure groups such as Anti-Apartheid, Amnesty International or any of the more aggressive charities can increase a Member's level of information — so long as his interest is not confined to the annual cocktail party.

Clearly MPs are in a position to influence. Their Parliamentary colleagues, Ministers, the electors, world opinion are all subject to a slight deflection in course, a minute mutation in colour of opinion. MPs are all in a position to do this. Whether these tiny shades of pressure have any real effect on the shape of events is another matter. To some extent it depends upon the effort a Member is prepared to put in to bringing about changes, how successful he is.

The excuse that Parliament does not work is one way of explaining why Members of Parliament seldom achieve anything dramatic in the way of a legislative coup. But the excuse can look thin if the activities of some MPs are taken as an example of the way in which the Parliamentary system can be used to achieve positive results. Tam Dalyell is a perfect example of a Member who, according to his colleagues, works tirelessly to defeat or promote legislation. According to one lobby man Dalyell killed the Anglo-French Swing Wing project almost single-handed.

Referring to Tam Dalyell, Jeremy Bray says: 'There is much the ordinary Member can do.' However, he was keen to emphasise the importance of having a strong lobby in support. 'It does depend whom he represents,' says Bray, 'powerful interests are more easily represented,' even if they are commercial interests. But this can just as well apply to non-MPs.

As an MP Tam Dalyell is an exception. If Parliament works for him it is because he is prepared to put more than the average amount of energy into his lobbying and his research. Clearly Parliament does not fail to 'work' simply because the channels for getting things done do not exist, but rather because they have become silted up. The effort now required to get anything done is so great that MPs get tired out in the process. For a Member of Parliament to initiate a reform or to change legislation he has to be exceptionally determined, extremely patient, ruthlessly persistent and lucky to boot: he should know the right ears to whisper into and be able to mobilise support both inside and outside the House if necessary. On top of all this it helps if he has a newsworthy case. Seldom wonder if most of the activities of back-benchers consist of negative attempts to outmanoeuvre Ministers in the Chamber, or destructive speeches in the press when at best their activity has no more effect than sinking a pin into a blancmange.

Activity in itself is not always necessary for an achievement to be registered. Dafydd Wigley, a Plaid Cymru MP, says that between 1966 and 1970, 'Some things were achieved simply because Gwynfor Evans was in the House. I am sure that the fact that he was an MP enabled us to get their ear.' Wigley was referring in particular to the Labour Government's decision to build the Royal Mint in Wales. But this could easily have been due to the fact that the Labour Government was anxious to keep the support of the Member for a once Labour seat for some of its more awkward legislation.

Swap agreements of this kind are common in coalition situations where the Government needs support from outside its own party.

The power of an individual MP to achieve anything must depend on the energy he is able to apply and the forces he is able to muster in any given situation. Naturally it should not be made too easy for every dilettante to push his little whims on to the Statute Book. We are over-burdened with finicky pieces of legislation as it is. Paradoxically the improbability of an MP ever getting a real piece of reforming legislation on to the floor of the House, never mind the Statute Book, tends to encourage back-benchers' interest in small legislative loopholes. Michael English is one MP who devotes his creative time to removing some of the loopholes that alone have made our laws tolerable. During the Labour period of office (1966–70) he achieved the distinction of amending the tax law so that barristers in their last year of work were no longer allowed the earnings of that year tax free. That he got this through a House full of barristers is even more amazing than that he should have thought of it in the first place. It is perhaps fortunate that Michael English is prevented from initiating legislation on a larger scale.

It may be disheartening to be prevented from conducting

one's own personal revolution on the floor of the House; but one of the happier aspects of our restrictive system is that the lunatic ideas as well as the worthwhile ones get lost. As John Pardoe says, however, 'it could be a lot easier and still be safe' for the individual Member of Parliament to make some constructive contribution to the running of society. As it is, the role is mainly negative. Parliament is a sanction house and most of the sanctions are a walk-over for the Government.

Clearly much of the onus for this does lie with individual MPs. But they are limited by other factors. It is a common accusation that if they were not so concerned with their own career prospects, they could obstruct the actions even of their own Front Bench. Indeed there are some indications that courage would be a welcome ingredient in the House of Commons soup. But the chances are that any Member operating too boldly would soon fall out of favour. Once a Member has offended, he is less likely to be able to bend ears. And influence is a major part of the MP's opportunity for positive achievement. Condemned then to a somewhat female role in the great system of the British Parliament, the MPs must be careful not to offend. Marcus Lipton, who named Kim Philby as the 'Third Man' in the Burgess and Maclean case, says that 'for a long time afterwards' his Parliamentary life was 'made very difficult indeed'. Only years later when Philby defected to Moscow himself, did Lipton emerge from the dark cloud of disaffection which so obstructed constructive relations with his colleagues in the House.

This chapter has been about the power of the individual MP. It is doubtful whether this is any greater now than it ever has been. Two things in particular have changed since the Reform Bill Parliament of the last century. One is the flow of work and the increasing complexity of Government activity. The other is the growth in the domination of parties in the Parliamentary system as a whole. It is the party above all that governs the behaviour of MPs in all the workings of Parliament. The relationships of Members with the Executive is inextricably linked with their relationships with party. If Parliament does not work it is not only because Government is all-powerful:

not solely because MPs lack the courage to put their own House in order. Rather it is because all the exchanges which take place between the Member and the Executive do so within the straitjacket of party.

POWER OF THE PARTY AND CONSCIENCE OF THE MAN

'The essence of the constitution is party,' Brian Walden, MP.

The Party in Parliament

During the 1964–66 Parliament someone coined the term 'lobby fodder'. The description caught on. It was the start of the disrespect for Parliament which is the hallmark of present-day politics. It was not the first insult to be levelled at MPs but it was the most apt for some time. Members of Parliament were at this time filing down the lobbies to cast their votes for and against the new Labour Government in the biggest rush of three-line Whips within recall.

This was the Parliament in which Labour held a majority of four. According to a remark made by Harold Wilson to Herbert Morrison a small majority was what he had hoped for, on account of the fact that it would be good for party discipline. In the preceding two years leading up to the General Election, Wilson had managed to hold his party together in a manner unprecedented during the past strife torn decade. Even he, however, could hardly have hoped for a majority so small.

So fragile was the majority that Members were brought into the lobbies from their sick beds. Jokes were made about the stretcher vote. Members who were gravely ill slept in make-shift dormitories rigged up in Ministers' offices where oxygen and medical attention were administered during the long winter of all night sittings. One Member was driven into the precincts of the House in an ambulance so that his vote could be recorded. No wonder Labour Members demanded that proxy voting should be introduced. Meanwhile the Whips watched anxiously for fog at airports, rail delays and for news of heart attacks or influenza. Lobby fodder may have been an insulting term but who, under the circumstances, could argue with its validity.

Even when the crisis of the knife edge majority was over after 1966 the accusation continued to be levelled. Press and public could not get it out of their heads that Members of Parliament were the pawns of the Party Whips. As the legislation went on at an unprecedented rate and much of it contrary to Labour Party policy the screams grew louder. Labour Members writhed under a scathing barrage of press comment but remained remarkably docile. The training period of the small majority had done its work. Loyalty was now ingrained into the Parliamentary Labour Party. In spite of the fact that there was now a working Labour majority of nearly one hundred, the signs of rebellion were markedly absent, on the surface at least.

Although rebellion was to break out later, that particular period did more than anything to draw public attention to the power of the Whips. If a Government really wants to put legislation through the House in the face of every one it puts out a three-line Whip.

The power of the Executive has reached its ultimate point. It is recognised that the individual Member of Parliament is powerless in the face of the Government; and that powerlessness is related to the power of the Whips.

The Foundations of Whipping Power

Before becoming a Member of Parliament the individual must win the approval of a political party. That approval, as we have seen in Chapter 2, Part I, depends upon at least a pretence of common viewpoint. The individual agrees in principle and on the whole with the policies of the party he joins. The privilege which is open to the Member of any party is to amend and contribute to that party policy at the appropriate time. The Labour Party, it should be remembered, is the strictest of all in that it demands of its candidates that they put party policy before their own views on each occasion. No one surely can pretend that before he goes into Parliament he does not know what to expect.

The alternative to party sponsorship is to stand as an Independent; but the day of the Independent in British politics is past. If it ever had a day, it was certainly not in the twentieth century. Party politics now dominate the electoral scene. To emphasise this and the increasing trend towards party domination which most Members agree is occurring, the name of the party now appears beneath the name of the candidate on the ballot paper.

Recent work has shown that four-fifths of the electorate always support the same party at elections and that 90 per cent have an image of themselves as being closer to one party than to the others. In the face of this, what hope has an Independent candidate, even if he can afford to stand?

Of the true Independents, ex-Members fighting their own constituencies have been proved the most successful. Even before World War II there were few Independent candidates. Of these only six obtained 20 per cent of the vote. It was only during the war years when one or other major party failed to put up a candidate that Independents were elected in any numbers. In 1945 a number of former Members stood as Independents and seven were successful. Four of these lost their seats in 1950 and the only memorable successes since then have been that of the late S. O. Davies in 1970, Dick Taverne in 1973 and Ted Milne in 1974 (when more Independents stood than usual).

As time goes on chances get harder for Independents. Parties put their point of view to the electorate through the mass media, through advertising, newspapers and expensive literature. What the Government is doing and what the Opposition is saying fills the papers in relative states of distortion and omission every day. What chance has the Independent except to stand on issues of paralysing simplicity; anti-Common Market, CND or anti-Harold Wilson. What can the individual promise compared to the party? What has the Independent to say that competes with the extravagant promises of the party manifesto? Party has become, as Brian Walden says, 'the essence of the constitution'. And, in Parliament at least, its instrument is the Whipping system. The Whipping system is a requisite of the party system, and the rise in power and authority of the Whips has accompanied the rise in the dominance of the party. Traditionally, the role of the Government Whip is that of adviser to the Cabinet on the level of support to be found within the Parliamentary party for the various items of legislation planned; also advice is given as to the availability of Members to attend debates and subsequent divisions. Members are obliged to inform the Whips office when they are to be away from the House and frequently it will be the task of the area Whip to persuade the Member to attend if it is necessary to keep numbers up.

Opposition Whips keep the same functions. What is less traditional but of increasing importance is the authority Whips wield in the instructions they send out to Members. The instructions contained in the Whip are the strategic command of the party for its tactical warfare. They are issued one week ahead at a time. The Government decide the business by the Thursday of the week preceding and the Whips are circulated to Members on that day or on the Friday. If the Whip is a three-liner it will probably include the words 'Your presence is essential' and give the time of the division. This will be underscored three times. Alternatively the Whip may also request attendance at the debate or sometimes 'throughout the debate'. If the Whip is a two-liner the Member is free to absent himself so long as he has 'obtained a pair'. The words 'Your attendance is particularly requested' are usually a feature of a two-line Whip. They will be underscored twice. If the Whip is a single-liner, the words 'Your attendance is requested' are a probable formula — underlined once.

Not only then do Whips advise the party leaders on the level of support, but they arrange the level of support through their weekly Whipping instructions to Members. The instructions vary according to whether there is to be a free vote, a two- or three-line Whip. The interpretation of a three-line Whip is generally that it is a summons to attend. Three-line Whips are issued with increasing frequency and few Members would appear to be in doubt as to their significance.

The old-fashioned view on the meaning of the three-line Whip was expressed by Quinton Hogg in a television interview at the time of the Profumo scandal. A three-line Whip was to be put out for the vote of confidence in Macmillan's Government, following the revelation that John Profumo had lied to the House over his relationship with Christine Keeler. Naturally the Government did not want to have a vote of No Confidence and so uncertain were they of their support that the three-liner was issued. Much was made of this in the television interview; so much, in fact, that Hogg was led to say: 'Whips only tell Members to come and not how to vote.' Nigel Birch, at the end of the debate preceding the Vote of Confidence, drew attention to the words spoken on television. 'I call the Whips to witness,' he said, 'that I at least have attended.' He then abstained.

George Wigg, who very actively stirred the Conservative Party confusion over the whole period of the scandal attacked Hogg's interpretation saying: 'The three-line Whip is the final appeal to loyalty on party lines and Lord Hailsham knows it.' The argument persisted and Hogg, not unsupported, said after the vote that the 27 Conservative abstentions proved him right. 'A direction how to vote would be, I conceive, a direct contempt for the House,' he said, adding, 'and certainly the Party I belong to has always taken that view.'

Indeed the parties do view the matter differently. The use that is made of the powers of the Whip varies consistently from gentle pressures on the part of the Conservatives to harsher threats by the Labour Whips. It has been said that the Labour Party has forced cohesion in Parliament on to the Conservative Party. Certainly the rise in the fortunes of the Labour Party has been accompanied by those of Whips in general. Whips were originally unpaid officers outside the realm of the code of collective responsibility. The entry of the Government Whips in 1964 into the ambit of that code put them irrevocably on the side of the Executive. Instead of advisers to the Cabinet from the ranks of Members, they have become the creatures of party leadership. Now that Opposition Whips receive a salary the same applies to them.

The position of the Government Chief Whip was recently referred to by the Boyle Committee in the following terms: 'We consider that the Government Chief Whip of the House of Commons should be paid at the highest level in the intermediate scale for Ministers. We are convinced that this is right, bearing in mind his heavy responsibilities in respect of Parliamentary business and as political adviser to (though not a Member of) the Cabinet.' Boyle recommended a salary of £9,500 for the Government Chief Whip. This is paid in addition to a salary in respect of other duties as a Member of Parliament, of £3,000. Even an ordinary Government Whip is now paid an extra £4,000 in addition to his basic £3,000.

The recognition of the Opposition as Her Majesty's Opposition dates back to 1937. It is considered an aspect of good Government that the situation of Opposition with Government should be equalised as much as possible. There is a long way to go, before this happens. Shadow Ministers, for instance, are hopelessly out of touch with the issues being handled by their opposite number on the Government Front Bench. Whether it would improve the chances of getting better Opposition or simply improve the opportunities for further collusion to let Shadow Ministers in on Ministry details is another question. It relates, however, to the situation whereby the Leader of the Opposition is now paid a salary of £9,500 in addition to his Parliamentary allowance and whereby his Chief Whip is also paid a salary of £7,500 over his Parliamentary allowance. The importance of good whipping by the Opposition was clearly seen by Lord Boyle and his Committee when they decided that two other Opposition Whips to be nominated by the Chief Whip would be allowed to receive the standard Whips' salary as paid to ordinary Government Whips.

Whips are now a part of the paraphernalia of Government: their allegiance to the leaders of their parties sealed by the nature of their appointment; party leaders after all choose Whips, and it is often a job for their faithful friends. The power of the Whip is proxy power for the man who holds the strings; through the Whip the party leader runs his party in the House of Commons. The power is not omnipotent; in fact, the extent of it depends on the degree to which Members of Parliament are prepared to buckle under. The power of the Whips is, however, insidious and all-embracing. It is only prevented from achieving its ends when enough Members of Parliament are pushed to the threshold of tolerance sufficient to rebel in such a way as to endanger the party leadership.

Threats and Cajolery: How the Whips Work in Practice

The relationship between party leadership and Members of the Parliamentary party is one of delicate balance of the ultimate threat. Most of the time these threats are veiled; but on two occasions during the Labour 1964–70 Administration they were revealed.

The first occasion was shortly after the General Election of 1966. A row over D Notices was responsible for a rebellion in the Parliamentary Labour Party. At a stormy meeting of the PLP, Wilson threatened Labour Members with Dissolution of Parliament. This is the ultimate threat of the Prime Minister; but it was not the fact that the threat was uttered which stunned Labour Members so much as the terms in which it was put. This was the infamous dog licences speech. Wilson reminded Labour Members that they sat in the House only through the grace of the Labour Party. He said: 'All I say is "watch it". Every dog is allowed one bite, but a different view is taken of a dog that goes on biting all the time. If there are doubts that the dog is biting not because of the dictates of conscience but because he is considered vicious, then things happen to that dog. He may not get his licence renewed when it falls due' (Parliamentary Labour Party Meeting, March 2nd, 1967). The threat worked. Labour Members recently elected to office were not ready to see glory slide away so soon; while the storm in the press lashed on, their anger died to a murmur. Only one Labour MP, Hugh Jenkins, a persistent rebel, saw the true situation. He said: 'Harold's got it wrong. It's we who licence him, not he who licences us.'

But Labour Members lived with the indignity of that reference for three years before bringing their own ultimate sanction to bear. After several years in office they may have felt that the risk of bringing the Government down was no longer too great. The issue was, however, central to the credo of the Labour Party in that it concerned the power of the Trades Unions. In Place of Strife, the controversial White Paper proposals for taming the Trade Union movement divided the Labour Party. Half the representation in the PLP is Trade Union sponsored. Had the Government gone ahead with its Bill these Members would have wrecked the Labour majority. In spite of the fact that the Bill could have got through with Tory support, Wilson was not prepared to risk it. He knew his Party. This time it was not only the Parliamentary Party that he had to deal with but the Party as a whole. Rather than threaten dissolution as he had done in the vicious dogs speech, the Prime Minister backed down to save his own position.

As one Labour ex-Minister said to me over this issue: 'If he has threatened us with Dissolution, it would simply have been a matter of the Chairman of the Party getting into a faster car and reaching the Palace before him to tell the Queen that the Parliamentary Party wished to elect a new leader.'

In February 1972 the Conservative Party faced a comparable situation. Rebellion within the Party over the European Community Bill was severe enough to suggest a possible defeat for the Government in the House. Ted Heath warned recalcitrant back-benchers in a series of personal interviews that the Government would have to resign if defeated on the Bill's second reading.

His method of working was more discreet than Wilson's. But it produced a tougher response. The late Sir Gerald Nabarro was one of the more determined anti-marketeers to refuse the interview with his Prime Minister. He is understood to have told Heath's emissaries that the Prime Minister and himself were well enough acquainted with each other's European views.

In a speech in Croydon the night before the debate Sir

Gerald challenged Mr. Heath to repeat his warnings publicly. He also added, 'If we suffer the calamity of the loss of Mr. Heath by resignation there need not, and in my judgment will not, be a General Election. The Conservative Party,' he added, 'had always been greater than any of its Members.'

Those are the ultimate threats from both sides which guide the Whips in their task. They depend upon the threshold of tolerance which once reached will bring about a crisis of conscience in the Member. Fortunately for their sanity most Members have a fairly high threshold on many matters. Conscience is something which is offended on one issue for one Member and on another for someone else.

As Brian Walden says: 'Conscience is dependent on transient factors, often personal reasons. Nobody's record in this place proves them a man of conscience.'

A conscience derived from personal experience can indeed cause a Member of behave untypically. A right-wing Conservative who lost a relative through Capital Punishment behaved untypically when he voted for the Abolition of Capital Punishment. A left-wing Member, normally a Radical and a Progressive, voted against Abortion Law Reform; behaviour related to the fact that his wife is unable to bear children.

Other exercises of conscience can concern Members' special interests. Strong feelings on subjects usually result from some extensive experience of the issues involved. Conscience may, in these cases, determine that a Member should disregard the instructions of the Whip. Where conscience is involved the system of priorities changes. Where it is not involved, the power of the Whip is at its greatest.

The power of the Whip is exercised with varying intensity. Likewise the susceptibility of Members to the various pressures or rewards varies. Some people dislike any call other than that of their own conscience. It was John Gorst who said to me: 'One is expected to have a strong sense of party loyalty. I resent this more than words can say. It seems to be an affront to my integrity.'

Integrity indeed is one quality which politicians are suspected of lacking. Loyalty is equally highly regarded as a human attribute and integrity is after all only another form of loyalty. However, integrity is often a loyalty to oneself and to one's own sense of right and wrong. Voting in Parliament is, in fact, a conflict of loyalties. If self, party policy, Government or Whipping instructions or constituency interests, and in many cases other interests too, are all involved in the simple decision of which way to vote in a two-way lobby, it may be easier in the end to follow the Whip!

Yet the first loyalty that the Whip demands is that to party. This nebulous sense of loyalty is accepted by some and not by others. In the Conservative Party it is a code which operates less emphatically than in the Labour Party, but on the other hand Conservatives regard loyalty as more of law of nature; in the Labour Party, loyalty often has to be enforced.

Rewards and Punishments

The varying techniques of blackmail and bribery with which loyalty is strengthened are more effective under some circumstances than others. For instance, the varying rewards of loyalty include the chance of Ministerial positions; a piece of unstated blackmail which helps to keep younger Members in order. Records of the rebellions which have taken place in the past twenty-five years show that rebels tend to be mostly drawn from amongst the younger, and often newer Members. A threat to promotion chances must help to quieten the potential young Turks.

One of the great strengths of the Whips in the Government Party is well known as the payroll vote. As Norman Atkinson put it: 'There are one hundred Members in the Government, and a further one hundred who are hoping for jobs in the next re-shuffle or the one after. In a Parliamentary party of three hundred and fifty, the payroll men are in the majority.' Ministers are, of course, bound by collective responsibility. If they disagree with Government policy they are honour-bound to resign before registering their protest. Ministerial resignations are not, however, frequent. The tendency to want to hold on to power while one has it is no doubt stronger than most other impulses.

Rebellion is undoubtedly a gamble which can in the end turn out to be more of an advantage than a snag. A Member may be involved in outright rebellion against one administration and receive a Ministerial post from the next. It is a question of backing the winner. There are numerous examples of men in politics today who did just this. Harold Wilson was a rebel once. Likewise there are Conservatives, like Peter Kirk, who frequently rebelled during the fifties and who are Ministers today. Peter Kirk was Whip for the Conservative rebels over Suez shortly after his debut to the House. 'I think it did me a great deal of good,' is his verdict. 'At least,' he says, 'it got me known.' This sort of notoriety is perfectly all right in the right place. Peter Kirk is one of those whom history will vote is on the right side of the issue and he is lucky enough to have out-lived his major opponents in terms of political life.

The pages of political literature are sprinkled with the names of those who gambled and won, like Churchill, the highest stakes. If Harold Wilson casts a worried eye in the direction of Roy Jenkins' rebellion over the EEC issue, it may be because he was himself a successful rebel before he became Prime Minister.

Even so, the indications are that politicians with their eyes on plums do not rebel until it is of advantage to them to do so. Thus the more consistent rebels are usually those who have given up any idea of a high office, or who are not in any case looking for a ministerial career.

Ministerial position is not, as we have seen, solely the reward of good behaviour, nor is it the only reward. There are lesser but equally lucrative positions to be attained. The numerous plums, large and small, range from the job of Speaker which has a salary equal to the Prime Minister, to that of a minor Whip. They include such positions as Attorney-General, Lord Chancellor, Comptroller of Her Majesty's Household or Chairman of Ways and Means to name only a few.

If the prospect of Ministerial position helps to keep younger men in the power of the Whips, these kinds of rewards can be used as carrots held out to those who have given up hope of becoming Ministers. Lest anyone should become embittered or turn idle hands to evil work, there are a number of minor rewards in the form of patronage. Peerages, knighthoods, baronetcies and various honours are usually awarded for long and loyal service.

In the Labour Party rewards are given on retirement in the form of peerages. The Conservative Party, the tendency to give knighthoods to sitting Members after long service has produced the group known as the Knights of the Shires. This group of faithful Members from safe seats in the backwoods of Tory England have been rewarded as much for their services as to placate the sections of the party they represent.* There are persistent rebels among them. This is another example of the fact that rebellion can also bring its rewards so long as it is done in the right way. Rewarding rebels is one sure way of defusing their mischief circuit.

The Whips have no certain influence on the distribution of honours in Parliament but there is no doubt that they are consulted. A favoured Member may be asked if he would like an honour for a wealthy contributor to his constituency funds, or to a faithful local supporter. If there is a big black book somewhere, and where better than the Whips of Office, then it is sure to be consulted on these occasions.

The Whips are regularly consulted on the distribution of short-term favours such as membership of Parliamentary delegations. Official delegations to foreign countries, or those to alliance conferences such as NATO or the council for Europe are decided by the Whips. Ostensibly the Speaker decides but in fact he bases his decision on the lists of recommended names he receives from the Whips' offices. It has been observed by several Members that these small gifts go to some people more often than others; and to persistent rebels, almost never at all.

Other invitation lists include invitations to official functions, lunches with the Queen, dinners at the Foreign Office; and it has even been suggested that London hostesses ask the Whips'

* *Jackson Rebels and Whips* — page 250.

Offices for names to be included in their lion-hunting dinner parties.

Quite naturally, young men who want to get places will see to it that their name appears on as many of these lists as possible. The greatest weapon of the Whips is exclusion; socially conscious individuals do not like to be excluded and therein lies much of the insidious power of the Whip.

One of the disciplinary uses of exclusion is deprivation of the Whip. This is used far more frequently by the Labour Party than by the Conservative. In fact the Conservatives have not deprived a Member of the Whip since 1942 and only once earlier in this century. In the same period of time ten Labour Members have been deprived of the Whip. Only one Labour Member in that time resigned the Whip voluntarily, whereas sixteen Conservatives resigned. Conservatives say that resigning the Whip is 'only grander than having it withdrawn'.

The effect, whether the Whip is removed or is resigned, tends to be the same. It is a form of exclusion from the happy collusive club.

Losing the Whip could sound like a ticket to freedom. In fact it is far from that. The Whip is both jailor and wet-nurse to Members of Parliament. Once they have received the Whip Members can decide which night to take their girl-friend out to dinner or their wife to the theatre. More important, they know which business is important and exactly where it comes on the schedule. The value of help given by the Whips is shown by the use that is made of them by genuine Independents. For instance, Bernadette Devlin took the Labour Whip for a time.

A Whipless Member loses the opportunity of voting with his colleagues over issues in which they would normally have his support. Moreover he also loses the opportunity to be nominated for Committees of the House. These nominations, both for Standing Committees and for Select Committees, are made through the Whips. Naturally Whips exclude Members who are effectively no longer an operating Member of the Parliamentary Party.

The exclusion can take other forms. Whipless Members

have at times been treated coldly by their colleagues. Some mind this more than others. So often, rebellious characters are the sort of people who can live without the constant approval of their fellows.

Exclusion from their own Parliamentary Party is a disadvantage to a Whipless Member in that he is also precluded from participating in any of the internal meetings. He may quite often receive copies of the Whip from his friends and in the same way hear gossip about what is going on at party committees and meetings. Nevertheless he is no longer a Member of the Parliamentary Party and for that reason is prevented from exerting any pressure or bringing any influence to bear within his own party.

Most Members who lose the Whip only do so for a period. Usually they regain it before the end of the Parliament and are re-adopted by their local parties. Recently Members tend to be punished by suspension rather than withdrawal, probably for a period of a month. During this time if anything important happens the MP may not get to hear of it, except through his friends. The normal channels for the flow of information is the Whip. Government and Opposition Whips frequently consult each other and when there is new accommodation available or something special like a flight in Concorde to be arranged, then they will communicate with each other, suggest names: naturally these will exclude any Whipless Members.

Worse than having the Whip withdrawn is the ultimate punishment of expulsion. In the last twenty-five years no Conservatives and six Labour Members have been expelled. The first five Labour expulsions took place during the reds under the beds panic that swept Europe after World War II. Four of the expelled Labour Members were thus disciplined on the basis of recurrent sympathising with Communism. The Labour Party could hardly afford to be associated in the public mind with Communism and the four Members were expelled for a series of offences ranging from remarks in Parliament to speeches made outside the House, articles written, and telegrams sent to quasi Communist alliances. One of these Members, Konni Zilliacus, was later brought back into the Labour

Party though not without opposition. He represented Gorton until his death, but was disciplined on at least one occasion after his return.

The fifth expulsion was for aiding the Conservatives, and the sixth was that of Desmond Donnelly on the formation of his Democratic Party in 1969.

Apart from Zilliacus, none of the expelled MPs ever returned to the House, though all stood in their old constituencies immediately following their expulsion, but as Independents. Clearly no one can be expelled from his Party and continue to represent it in Parliament. Even when a Member crosses the floor, however, he is still entitled to sit for his constituency until Parliament is dissolved.

Such extreme cases are rare. There have, in recent years, been more cases of Front Bench disciplining than those applying to back-benchers. The removal of Enoch Powell from the Front Bench of the Tory Party for his seditious racialist speeches, the sacking of Dr. Jeremy Bray on the publication of his book criticising Whitehall, the removal of Richard Marsh and many others who have disagreed with Mr. Wilson, might be considered as forms of discipline by the party leadership. Discipline is much tougher in the Labour Party and was particularly so under Harold Wilson, who used every means of pressure and enticement in the book to keep order among his Parliamentary party.

Historically, the Labour Party has more reason to be tough. It is formed from a coalition of Trade Union groups, with a *soupçon* of socialist intellectuals. During the fifties it tore itself to shreds in public, over everything from clause four to nuclear disarmament. Yet, curiously during this period in opposition, it suffered fewer Parliamentary rebellions than the Conservative Party. Loyalty is of course more important, when a party is in power: but at the same time back-benchers are more likely to feel the need to defend party policy against the pragmatic practices of Government. During the opposition phase a party Member has more opportunity of exerting influence on his colleagues. Once the party is in power illusions that all Members of the Governing Party are equal fade away.

Formal rebellion is often the only real method of drawing public attention to the fact that there is dissent in the ruling party.

Sometimes the Whips welcome a measure of formal dissent. On a touchy issue it can be a political advantage to a party to show that a faction disapproves of its Government's actions. The reason why Norman Atkinson and his *Tribune* Group colleagues so often got away with their abstentions and other Whip-defying practices, was that they represented a voice in the PLP which held out for the adopted policy of the party against the necessarily pragmatic actions of the Government. On issues like prescription charges and immigration control Labour MPs went quietly into the lobbies or equally quietly stayed away. It can only have been in the interest of the party as a whole that someone should be seen to have a conscience: so the left had their predictable rebellion. On the other hand the charge is often levelled against the rebels, that they were only enabled to express their righteousness because other Labour Members were willing to go into the Government lobby to keep Labour in power, even at the cost of facing constituency wrath and their own guilty conscience at the end of the day.

This, of course, is where the crunch comes for all middle of the road men. The Labour Party, having spent thirteen near disastrous years in fratricidal strife, managed to keep quiet for long enough to get elected to power. With a name for internal disunity and national bankruptcy to live down, Labour under Harold Wilson had to do two things. One was to look united and the other was to get the economy right. The pragmatism of Harold Wilson's policies was frequently at variance with the adopted policy of the party: but in order to show that Labour Government could work, the party in general, and the MPs in particular were, at first, prepared to stick their loyalty where their principles had been and toe the pragmatic line.

After the defeat of 'In Place of Strife', however, rebellion was more marked. It was clear from the way the Government was forced to back down over this issue that back-benchers could control the Government if they wanted to. Attitudes in the Labour Party are such that a future Labour Government will be forced to take more notice of party policy, if only because the party as a whole has shown that it will not sanction such whole sale neglect of its wishes.

The Party in the Constituency

Constituency parties are increasing their level of interest in the voting patterns of their Member. The heavy-weight power of the party machine in Parliament may be useful for coercing and cajoling MPs: but where local feelings are concerned the Member has to look carefully at his grass roots support before voting. The Whip is the servant of the leadership and therefore of Executive or shadow Executive. The local party rightly regards itself as the sponsor of the Member in Parliament. If the Whip disregards grass roots opinion the Member may find himself in a cleft stick.

During the last period of Labour office Eric Heffer was heard to describe his Parliamentary colleagues as 'a load of ruddy kippers — two faces and no backbone'. He was referring to the habit of so many Labour Members of muttering rebellion behind the backs of Whips and Ministers, possibly telling their local party supporters how they were disgusted with the Government's activities and then meekly voting with the Whip.

Whichever way they voted, Members were in an awkward position. Some local parties blamed their Member for supporting the Government against party policy; others blamed their MPs for failing to support the Government against the Opposition. As Brian Walden says: 'Finding the right balance between all the various aspects of the Parliamentary job is essential for a Member's survival.' Finding the balance between the many factions of one's party is even harder.

This is particularly true of the Labour Party where there is less margin of tolerance for the independent view. In the last Government, the only Members who were able to vote against the Government or abstain with impunity were those whose local parties were entirely in support of them all the time and who were voting on party policy most of the time. Persistent Labour rebels, like the *Tribune* Group MPs, all have constituency associations as left wing as themselves. And, 'The left,' says Norman Atkinson, 'have never voted against adopted party policy although they have voted persistently against the Labour Government.'

But in other cases the local party supports Whip against MP. A very difficult situation, then, was the one in which the Labour pro-marketeers found themselves after the second Wilson *volte-face* on EEC Entry. Dick Taverne, Leo Abse, Jack Dunnet, Tom Ellis and Wil Edwards all faced angry local parties. Leo Abse's Young Socialists called for him to be reprimanded. The Welsh Labour Party Executive recommended that Wil Edwards be replaced at the next General Election. Edwards himself, however, claims that his local party association 'are always very good on such occasions'. Dick Taverne was given a narrow vote of no confidence. The five were in the unfortunate position of being right and then wrong on the same issue in quick succession.

In a marginal, however, internal party rows can be fatal to the position of the ruling party. In safe seats, a second candidate ostensibly of the same party can split the vote and still not affect the final result. For instance in Stratford upon Avon, in 1966, a section of the local party put up an Independent Con-Conservative candidate. Angus Maude, the official Tory, had been at that time the centre of a party row of national proportions. The local organisation was divided but a majority continued to support him. The Independent Conservative dented Maude's majority by a mere 1,733 votes, leaving him with 9,427. By 1970, troubles forgotten and with the wind of change behind it the majority was up to 16,713.

Curiously, most rows are about the Member's position in relation to the party nationally. They are about party political issues and not about local constituency issues. Thus if the candidate is politically in tune with his local party he will stay happily related to them.

The pressure from the constituencies is, however, growing. Brian Walden says that in the Labour Party at least 'the constituency party is taking more of a direct interest in the way its Member votes'.

At every stage in his career the local party exerts a powerful influence on the Candidate/MP's political judgment. Just how much of an influence depends upon the association and the individual. But during selection the applicant will bend his views to suit public leanings; and during the subsequent elections, alter the emphasis of his views to suit the factions of his local party.

Money is at the centre of the problem of the relationship of candidate to local party. Grass roots not only means the mood of the people, but the money they pour into the coffers. Much of the financial support in all parties is raised locally. The Conservatives are slightly better off in that their agents are paid a salary from the central coffers. On the other hand the Tories are much richer than the other parties because they tend to attract richer Members who give larger donations. But a desire to keep money flowing may also bear on policy and the way a Member speaks and votes.

The local organisation also does all the work. At elections it is local party hand and leg power, as well as purse power which swings the party machine. A Member has to remember that a disgruntled association is less likely to work well than a satisfied one. In time the strength of the Members personality will make itself felt. A good, diligent and well loved Member is more likely to get away with dissident behaviour on major policy issues. But the level of personal support amongst constituency parties can always change unfavourably; enemies are easily made in politics.

Somewhere in all this there is a more sinister aspect. Local parties surely have the right to guide their Member. Also to make their views known to him. They have the same right as every constituent to make their individual protest felt. They have the right as party Members to remind the MP of party policy as agreed at national conferences. But how much should they insist on obedience to their whims?

The Labour Party makes a great mechanical effort to be democratic. To its credit it sometimes succeeds. Through the delegate system the local party is reasonably representative of its sources of support; but the Member, as Brian Walden says, is not a delegate. The Member is a representative, not only of the local party but also of the constituency. Is it justified, therefore, that the local party should assume that it speaks for the constituency as a whole? Should it try to force the Member to obey its wishes?

We have seen that the local party has a great deal of power in the selection of its candidate. The more massive the voting shift required to turn out the sitting Member, the greater the power of the local party organisation to control the way their Member behaves politically.

It can be argued that in seats with an overwhelming majority of one particular party, the local party is more representative of the constituency as a whole than in marginals. In such a situation the Member should bear in mind the response of the electorate to his political judgments rather more than the marginal MP. In reality the reverse is true. It is the MP for the marginal constituency who has to nurse his support the more carefully. He therefore cares more for the opinions of a large number of voters than his safely seated colleagues.

It is usually the MPs in marginals who spend the most time in their constituencies; who make the most speeches in the local press: who jump up and down most often in Parliament asking questions of local interest. It is a further paradox of the MP's relationship with his constituency that the marginal Member will more likely be crucified for making local political or personal errors than for disobeying the Whip. This being for the simple reason that it is the electors who hold the Whip hand.

Curiously enough it is the electorate who demand integrity from their Member. Whilst Whip and local party together will cry out for the Member to keep his party in power, the electors will judge him in the end for the promises he has stood up for against every pressure.

It is in the words of a Conservative Member that the situation is expressed most clearly. In remarking one day in the Chamber, 'Would it be proper to bring down the Government?' he was expressing the possibility of the final sanction which party politics no longer accepts as valid. No Member of Parliament will bring down his own Government: but until that threat is made real the power of the Whips is secure; and lobby fodder a fact of Parliamentary life.

Harold Wilson's remark about dog licences was for all its poor taste based upon solid ground. That many Labour Members lost their seats at the 1970 General Election was an indication that party supporters and voters will stand for fewer broken promises than Members of Parliament.

Brian Walden says of Parliament: 'Party is what this place is all about.' He is right, but the party is also the reality which conceals the lie — that there is such a thing as a mandate, that election promises count on either side of the House, that Governments represent the majority. Most Governments come to power with a Parliamentary majority obtained by a minority of the votes cast. At the same time the glib phraseology of the party manifesto is hardly a foundation for the decision-making of any administration. If Governments eat their manifestos within weeks of receiving the precious mandate and upset both their own party members and the voters who put them in, the coercion of the Whips is contrary to all the cornerstones of democracy: the whole principle of going to the country is made farcical.

Reform of the electoral system, whereby a more accurate reflection of voters' political diversity would be represented in the House, would certainly help: but without complementary reform of the system by which Members of Parliament vote there would be no long-term benefit. In the flexible political climate following the General Election of February 1974, MPs had high hopes of increased power for Parliament. But sadly this only emphasised the power of parties. If government legislation was to stand or fall upon minority support then consultation between Whips as to how their Members would vote was increased, and the power of the Whips grew correspondingly.

It was Richard Wainwright, re-elected Liberal Member for Colne Valley, who at this time stated that the new situation called for new procedure.

But old habits die hard. Too much attention focused by the media on the possibility of government defeat in the lobbies, ensures the importance of Whips and devalues the conscience of the individual Member. Even in the situation of a minority government the Executive retains its potency: the dangers to Parliament also increase, for no one seems to know for certain how many administrative decisions can take place behind its back.

If anyone can bring about the requisite changes, anyone who can protect the powers of Parliament against the might or sleight of hand of the Executive is its Members themselves.

3

LENS OF THE MEDIA

A Conservative Peer once remarked, in disparagement of news-paper men, that 'they are not the sort of chaps one would want to invite to one's house for the week-end'. Journalists are rarely gentlemen either by birth or by behaviour: getting the news can involve the use of distinctly ungentlemanly techniques and printing the truth is often a breach of well-bred discretion. Nevertheless politicians of gentle birth or otherwise are in no doubt of the power of the press. Whatever a Member of Parliament wishes to say, if it should be to an audience wider than that of the readership of *Hansard*, or that contained by a village hall, needs to be said via press, radio and television. Journalists are the medium through which politicians reach the bulk of their audience: the media themselves are the tools of power, the vehicle for the extension of influence. The media are the lens through which the public views its politicians.

Not all politicians are equally aware of the power of the media; not all are equally skilled in turning the news processes to their advantage. This is not surprising. Understanding and employing media to influence public opinion is a specialised technique around which an entire industry has grown up. Some have it more than others. Politicians have traditionally been the possessors of the sort of instinctive knowledge on which this technique is based: in other words, saying the right thing at the right time in order to gain the most impact, and wield the most influence.

Newsworthiness is an assessment of topicality and impact value: it depends among other aspects on the fame or position of the personalities involved. Some Members of Parliament are more newsworthy than others. Ministers are more newsworthy than back-benchers: some back-benchers more than others. One of the surprising aspects of being a Member of Parliament is that the job seems to carry with it a halo of instant limelight. MPs are newsworthy simply by the acquisition of the label MP. If they manage to make a topical or controversial remark, they cannot fail to attract publicity. On the other hand — if what an MP says is not newsworthy, however valid, it fails to reach the public at large.

The Press in the Constituency

Most Members first experience of the importance of the media in their political lives is in their constituency. Before he became MP for Brighton Kemptown, Bowden told me that an opinion poll placed him as the best locally known Conservative candidate in the country and his opponent Dennis Hobden as the best locally known MP. 'This,' says Bowden, 'was entirely because of the *Argus*,' which according to the same survey was the best read local paper in the country and the one carrying most news about its local politicians.

John Pardoe tells me that recognition of the Member is very important in rural areas; it tends also to be higher than in urban constituencies. 'In a recent survey,' he says, 'we found that 88 per cent of my constituents knew me by sight.' Press and television certainly play their part here, not only locally but nationally. Not all Members of Parliament receive equal attention from the national media however. Most Members are concerned to keep up the level of mentions they get in their own constituency and bother little with national politics. Tabling questions for Ministers is one of the standard Parliamentary devices for maintaining the flow of news locally. MPs seeking national notice also use the system with good effect. Ian Aitken, Political Correspondent of *The Guardian*, says: 'During the national newspaper strike the number of questions being tabled, dropped substantially.'

Not all Members of Parliament are falling over themselves to get publicity: but shunning the limelight is not a usual part of the business of influence. If an MP knows the techniques, he is in a very good position to carry his influence into a wider court than that of his constituency alone. Speeches by MPs can attract enormous attention; often more than Government statements. Enoch Powell is a man who is very well aware of the power of the press and who uses it ruthlessly for his own ends. Gerald Nabarro was not without success, and other backbenchers such as William Hamilton, Tom Dalyell, Michael Foot and Marcus Lipton quite regularly project their enthusiasms into the national arena. Any Member of Parliament who chooses to lead public opinion on a controversial issue, is bound to attract considerable attention not only in news value, but in the form of comment and debate. Controversy is the spice of journalism, and it is the best-known MPs who are most aware of this fact.

But the same controversy is less easily stirred by ordinary candidates or even ex-MPs. Eric Lubbock is a man who has used the media with noticeable success to achieve political ends. 'But, the press,' he says, 'are much less interested in what I have to say now than when I was an MP.'

The Press in Parliament

By a curious paradox the importance of MPs is a result of their newsworthiness rather than vice versa. Information is the lifeblood of democracy and Parliament has to be reported for this reason. It is for this reason that Parliament has its own corps of press men. There are gallery reporters and sketchwriters who record the caprices of the chamber: and there is the Parliamentary lobby that reports and comments upon the more elusive back-room currents of political life.

John Pardoe says: 'The lobby is a monstrous conspiracy to kid the British people that Parliament is important.' This may be an exaggeration: but the fact that newspaper proprietors see fit to pay for the teams of reporters and correspondents that form the Parliamentary lobby and the press gallery,* indicates that they consider Parliament important. Again, according to

* *The Press, Politics and the Public* by Colin Seymore Ure — Chapter 6 and 7 for the history of Parliamentary reporting.

Pardoe, the system perpetuates itself because 'the reporters have to justify their salaries and so they are committed to supporting the idea that Parliament and its Members are important'.

This strangely incestuous relationship has become a solid institution. The lobby is as important to the politicians as they are to it. Yet neither side much cares for the other: it is a reluctant symbosis. Ian Aitken says: 'It is very much a love-hate relationship.'

Hate has lately been less in evidence than love according to critics. The Parliamentary lobby has been under attack for sychophancy from other journalists and some MPs. This is partly a legacy of the way in which the Labour leaders used the lobby in their last period of office. According to Pardoe: 'Harold Wilson mercilessly used the lobby.'

Ted Heath is pathologically reluctant to speak to non-lobby journalists and the lobby is itself entirely dependent upon the co-operation of the politicians for its livelihood. The fact that there is a reverse dependence is less important. To live, the journalist must get his story and to succeed he must get the occasional scoop. He will not do this by abusing his sources of information at every opportunity. As Pardoe says: 'The chap at the top, in particular, who is so eager to keep all his lines open, is at the mercy of the politicians.'

In 1965 the *Sunday Times* attempted to break the hold of political leaders on the journalists who report their activities. A column headed Whitehall Correspondent written by Anthony Howard was to be the means. Whitehall Correspondent attempted to show the newspaper world that honest comment about the manipulations behind the scenes in the Ministries was possible. In a leader heralding the birth of the column the *Sunday Times* said: 'National Security excepted it is the job of newspapers to publish the secret matters of politics whether the secrets are the secrets of the Cabinet of Parliament or of the Civil Service.' If they can get hold of them. He who tells all is not on anyone's list of confidants. Howard's sources dried up one by one and the Whitehall Correspondent venture ended with his appointment as Washington Correspondent for the

Observer.* Poor Howard! Still a controversial figure of courage and considerable brilliance, he is now giving Harold Wilson some return fire as the Editor of the *New Statesmen*. His years in the cold ended, he can hardly have forgotten that it was Wilson as Prime Minister who gave the orders that resulted in the evaporation of his sources. The lesson given to Anthony Howard and the *Sunday Times* was valuable to the Wilson Administration. It kept the rest of the political journalists in fear of receiving the same treatment. Wilson was an expert in manipulating the lobby. Arthur Butler, who was at this time number one lobby man on the *Sketch*, says that Wilson often gave scoops to the Tory lobby men. 'He was,' says Butler, 'inclined to rely on those of us who were Labour men and throw all the titbits to people like Walter Terry in order to keep them sweet.'†

Does this mean that MPs can get exactly what they want into print on every occasion? The way in which MPs use the lobby varies according to the effect that is desired. Leaking is the name given to those off the record utterances which are nevertheless designed to end up in print: the unofficial statement uttered by a Junior Minister or a PPS, part of a wider manoeuvre. 'The journalist,' says Ian Aitken, 'has to be on guard against being used as a pawn: but there often is so little time that the story is written and in print before he realises that he has been had.'

It is the fact of correspondents too often falling for this kind of trick that lies behind John Pardoe's opinion that, 'there are people in the lobby who do not deserve the name of press men'. Gullibility is not one of the characteristics normally associated with the press: but politics is a curious world of double think, and not many of the lobby journalists are political thinkers. In fact one MP abuses them further by saying, 'many make a living out of a trade in gossip but they are intellectual eunuchs'. Certainly this does not apply to all or even most of the journalists in the lobby and the gallery.

* *The Press, Politics and the Public* by Colin Seymore Ure, gives a full account in Chapter 5.
  † Walter Terry was at this time political editor of the *Daily Mail*.

'Some of us,' says Aitken, 'are quite critical sometimes.' But all too infrequently unfortunately. The twilight world of the Parliamentary press man is the one area where the normally over critical facilities of good journalism are subdued. Parliamentary press work is *incubus succubus*. Words are too easily put into the minds of the lobby men. 'It is hard to tell,' says Aitken, 'whether a story is genuine or whether you are being planted with the seedling of some plot.'

But if politicians use the lobby so does the lobby use MPs. The lobby get to know in time who are the people to go to for a story. Some MPs are habitual leakers; Aitken calls them 'compulsive blabber mouths'. At the other times he says, 'the skill is to know who has an interest in telling you something'. MPs who have a grievance about something; others who have axes to grind are the ones to go to.

The lobby man's job is a watching, waiting game. 'Sometimes,' says Aitken, 'you get a sniff of something. It is a part of the art of the game to be sensitive to the moods of the House. You know something is up because Ministers may suddenly start appearing in the tea rooms and bars. For instance, when the gold crisis came,' Aitken says, 'the journalist realised before the MPs.'

The best lobby journalists build up good working relationships with the MPs. Likewise the MPs cultivate certain journalists. During the last period of Labour office, the collaboration between lobby journalists and Labour MPs was a source of constant embarrassment to Party leaders. Meetings of the PLP, held in private, were frequently so fully reported in the press that John Pardoe thinks: 'Some MPs were paid by journalists to report back.' Ian Aitken thinks it was most unlikely: but the possibility is very real, 'so full and detailed were some of the reports,' says Pardoe, 'that someone must actually have been taking notes at the meeting; and I cannot believe they would go to those lengths without being paid.'

So serious was the problem of Labour MPs leaking their own versions of PLP meetings to pressmen that the party leadership now holds official conferences for lobby correspondents after each meeting. According to Ian Aitken, two journalists — one from *The Guardian* and one from the *Telegraph* — were responsible for finally pressurising the Labour leadership into releasing official accounts of these meetings. Whether these accounts are any more acceptable than the reports of renegade MPs is another question. All that official reports do is make journalists' relations with the leadership smoother: it possibly also saves them some money. Once again the lobby is in the position of depending upon the official version of the malleable truths of politics. In repeating these, they strengthen the hand of officialdom even more; back-benchers are once again relegated to the position of commentators on the creations of their leaders.

The traffic of information continues at other levels. It is conducted for a variety of motives: editorial policy influencing journalists, as much as party and inter-party politics motivates MPs. Dog eats dog, is a fundamental rule. The relationship is purely a marriage of convenience and one distinctly lacking in more than a rough blanket of respect. Yet it is the latter which, on the part of the lobby men has earned them a name for sycophancy. The sycophancy is only the public cloak for its complete opposite. Journalists may have to live off the backs of politicians — the tax they pay in verbal gratitude — but their respectfulness is cloak for their lack of respect: the lobby does not like its subject matter.

Neither, according to Ian Aitken, do most lobby men have any interest in politics itself. It is easier, he maintains for a politically interested journalist to understand the machinations of politicians: 'Yet most lobby men,' he said, 'have no political views whatsoever.' Perhaps that helps to make them more objective, but Aitken does not think so. 'It breeds the attitude that politics does not matter. And this,' he adds, 'is also the general view in the country.' How much do the media influence the public attitude to MPs? Journalists' attitudes certainly help to mould the public attitude towards politics. Journalists are partly responsible for the low view held of MPs by the public. The emphasis of journalists on the trivia of Parliament, on the worst elements of political behaviour, downgrades politicians. The tongue in cheek, the deadpan approach only adds to the impression that politics and politicians alike are all universally insignificant. This contrasts directly with the main purpose of Parliamentary reporting — to show the importance of what goes on in the House.

Jealousy may be partly responsible for this. Journalists realise that by writing about politicians they give them importance. By emphasising trivia and not the things politicians care about and show they care about, the journalist can remove some of the effectiveness of the politician. Again this mitigates for the Minister and the party leader. His handouts at least protect him from complete demolition. His power keeps the toadies prose rosy where he is concerned.

Ordinary MPs are more in danger of being misquoted or trivialised. Why should a lobby man care if an obscure backbencher or an unsuccessful Parliamentary candidate cuts him dead?

Some MPs are trivial: but so are some Ministers and party leaders. Unfortunately the sycophancy tends to operate in favour of the more authoritative figures and less for those who wish to oppose the *status quo* of the Executive. Sycophancy is, however, noticeably absent in the tone of non-Parliamentary journalists. The Parliamentary lobby is under control for sound practical reasons of mutual survival: but outside commentators are not so dependent for their living on the court they play to leading politicians.

Harold Wilson was particularly militant towards the BBC for the very reason that he was unable to control the reporters who worked for the current affairs programmes. Where it is possible to make life very difficult for a Parliamentary reporter who becomes too critical — by denying him information and facilities for investigation — there is no sanction that can be placed on the outside journalist other than censorship. Attempts have been made to curtail the too critical activities of some journalists however. After agitation from leading Conservatives, in April 1971, two journalists were asked to leave the BBC's World at One programme on the grounds that they were too biased towards the left. (One was the luckless Howard.) These expulsions followed a sustained campaign by

Conservatives against so-called left wing bias in the BBC. Curiously, the programmes attacked by Heath and his colleagues were the same as those which had most enraged Harold Wilson, bringing screams of protest from his Ministers. No wonder lobby correspondents are sycophantic when politicians react so violently to any criticism of their policies.

Top brass politicians may have considerable influence on what newsmen say: but it is nothing to the control that reporters and editors have over the way politicians are projected. Harold Wilson owed his position as Prime Minister to the adulation of pressmen throughout 1963 and 1964. He impressed them and they made no secret of it. Positive talk about 'white hot technological revolutions' and the 'rise of the meritocracy', were welcome music to the ears of reporters and correspondents. Sick to death of the fudging and fiddling among the Members of the tired Tory Government, journalists were easy prey to the first Wilson magic. But if it was the press that put Wilson on a pedestal, it was again the press who brought him down. The D Notice affair was the first crack in the make-up. Harold Wilson showed himself autocrat and manipulator without shame. The press turned against him almost to a man: and from that moment his personal image as wonder worker and man of integrity began to fade. Pique removed the false glamour and revealed the god to be a tiny minded, short-sighted, over clever little man. From being a man who could do nothing but good, Wilson became, as at the behest of a wicked fairy — one who could only do harm. It is possible to trace the decline of Harold Wilson's popularity to the point where, after the D Notice affair and Wilson's failure to give Cecil King a peerage, the *Mirror* turned sour and went from eulogy into the attack. The fact that three-quarters of the national press supports Conservative rather than Labour interests, may also explain why the *Mirror*'s defection from the wonderman Wilson club had such a dramatic effect on Labour Party grass roots support.

As far as ordinary back-benchers are concerned, the focus of the press is a little off-stage. Government action and Opposition reaction take headline precedence over the mur-

murings of individual MPs. Yet, Ian Aitken says: 'The power of MPs has damn all to do with the way Parliament is reported.' This is true most of the time. Nevertheless the lobby is the creature of the Executive, and to attract its attention ordinary MPs have to cut such capers, that when reported they do nothing to improve their standing with the public.

Problems of Fully Reporting Parliament

It is a dedicated reader who gets far enough into his newspaper to peruse the Parliamentary report. Most of what people read in their papers about Commons debates is that which finds its way into the headlines, and often the front page. Television and radio again serve to highlight the most controversial point of debate and ignore the comments of moderate and thoughtful MPs. It may be argued that only the most pertinent remarks are worth reporting. However wise a speech a Member makes, unless it is earth shakingly controversial, no one really wants to be bothered with it. All the more power to the elbow of the pressman. He picks out the more savoury exchanges: his editor then carves it down some more, and finally all that remains of a long and reasonable argument are a few sharp remarks. These can do little except to enhance the public impression that the Commons is permanently at loggerheads and that MPs are of little significance beside their leaders, the big names of politics.

Committees are a growing area of Parliamentary work. Their importance is such now that the public are allowed in, as they are into debates. The trouble with all this is that although a number of persistent people or a favoured few who live in London and have the patience to queue, are able to witness the processes of legislation in action. It is true that political commentators draw out the more intresting events and also talk about back-room machinations to a certain extent.

However, this chat also tends to pick on the spicier happenings. In consequence, much of the events of Parliament and the behaviour of the representatives during the legislative process is lost to all but the keenest political student.

All this gives considerable weight to the arguments for letting radio into the Chamber of the House, and for that matter into the committees too. If it is argued that very few people would bother to watch a television channel devoted exclusively to Parliament, it can be argued again that surely this is the least that can be done to enable more of those who want to see Parliament in action to do so: and without the inevitably biased interpretation of intermediaries however objective they may be.

Arguments against television of the House include the allegation that MPs would behave extrovertly and cut even more capers to attract the attention of the cameras. Against this is the point that this already happens. Question Time, as has already been noted in a previous chapter, is a farce: and rendered so by MPs who are only questioning for the sake of publicity. Surely, if TV or radio relayed all the comments and events in the Chamber in the way that *Hansard* does now, but more dramatically, MPs would make no more than a general effort to be put on record: and better, the record would be more open to scrutiny than it is now to the few tired readers of the weekly *Hansard*.

If there are snags, they are the more general technical difficulties: TV reporting from the Chamber would require the probably intolerable use of lighting. But there is nothing against radio reportage direct from the Chamber.

A system of informing the electorate which depends upon the prior judgment of intermediaries, however responsible, is at best paternalistic and at worst risky. Now that the concentration of the press into the hands of a few interests is increasing, there is a danger that opinion will also become correspondingly concentrated. A wider availability of basic knowledge is essential if we are to avoid a further reduction in the power of back-benchers in favour of the Government, CBI, TUC and other big names. MPs must be seen to be more effective before they can be more effective. This is the first step in countering the slide towards totalitarianism, and to that extent we are all in the hands of the media.

Part III

GOLDEN PAVINGS

THE RATE FOR THE JOB

In 1970, a Member said in the Chamber of the House:

'We do not like discussing our own problems and difficulties because we know we are here to take care of the
problems and grievances and to look after the living
standards of our constituents . . . There is never a best time,
only a least objectionable time for considering the matter.'

The Member was talking about the remuneration of Members of Parliament. The subject was first voted on by Members
in the Parliament of 1912. It has been voted upon ever since at
intervals, and each time with reluctance and some public disapproval. Apart from co-operatives and certain boards of
directors, Members of Parliament are the only group who can
vote themselves a pay rise. While the rest of the nation is sub-
jected to productivity deals, wage bargaining or annual salary
increments, Members of Parliament can decide for themselves
whether or not they should be paid more.

Members do not decide the amount of their award — although they do discuss it, but only after a committee of review
is appointed. This then reports on pay and conditions and
makes a recommendation on the amount.

The Principles of Payment

The first recommended salary for MPs was the £400 a year
introduced to the House by Lloyd George in 1912. Introducing
it the Liberal Prime Minister said: 'When we offer £400 a year

as payment of Members of Parliament it is not a recognition of the magnitude of the service, it is not a remuneration, it is not a recompense, it is not even a salary. It is just an allowance, and I think the minimum allowance to enable men to come here, men who would render incalculable service to the State and whom it is an incalculable loss to the State not to have here, but who cannot be here because their means do not allow it. It is purely an allowance to enable us to open the door to great and honourable public service to these men.' — (Official Report, August 10th, 1911. Vol. XXIX, c1383.)

As Fred Peart said in the House on December 20th, 1971, referring to this quotation, 'Since then successive Governments of various political complexions have sought to widen representation in this House by increasing payments to Members.'

Indeed this is so: but the principle behind the debate about payment is still far from clear. In December 1971, said Mr. Peart, the £400 awarded by Lloyd George would be worth £2,600. At that time Members were earning £3,250 which, according to the Boyle Committee which had recently reported, was in 1971 worth £2,260 of its value at the time it was awarded — 1964.

So much for the effect of inflation on Members' salaries. But what of the principle of payment itself. The number of private incomes among our representatives would not be far fewer than in Lloyd George's day. Therefore the principle of paying Members should be open to less argument than in those days. Strangely however it is not, but whereas principle is now clear in that payment of some sort should be made, the issue has become clouded and confused by many other factors.

Thirty years ago, Viscount Samuel remarked: 'An unpaid legislature and an unpaid judiciary are things essentially aristocratic.' Commenting on that recently Charles Pannell said: 'We live in a democratic society. I can acquit the Rt. Hon. Gentleman in that he has not had my experience.' He was referring to his bank manager.

Democracy works both ways: once we begin to pay people, we begin to think in terms of what we are getting for our money. Members in turn begin to think about the expenses they incur while carrying out their duties. Then factors like additional earnings and tax deductible allowances begin to creep in to confuse the situation even more.

There is still an argument. It is not about whether Members should be paid at all but about how they should be paid. Members are presently self-employed. The trend, however, as Enoch Powell pointed out in the House, is 'to turn them into paid, salaried and pensioned employees'. Powell disapproves, but Norman Atkinson thinks that this should be done and as soon as possible. 'Members of Parliament should become paid employees of the State,' he says. Few of his colleagues would agree with him. Powell would certainly not agree with him. Many of Powell's views belong in a previous century; but the principle which he was supporting during the long exchanges over the Boyle Committee report in December 1971 is one central to the whole nature of our Parliament.

A Member of Parliament, says Powell, must 'be a person exercising his status at his own discretion and on his own responsibility'. The moment the MP becomes an employee of the State he is instantly less free, less self-responsible, less able to exercise his own discretion. The whole tendency of modern Government is to reduce this traditional status: to place the Member of Parliament on the footing of the State servant. The power of the Whip; the increasing heavy-handedness of local party organisation; the reduced significance of the open forum of the Chamber and the hustings in favour of back-room committees and media communications, are all a part of the trend towards the MP as cog in the Government wheel rather than the free, fearless voice of the people's representative.

The Boyle Committee reported in November 1971. It recommended that Members' salaries should be increased from £3,250 to £4,500 a year. It based its recommendation on a detailed assessment of the way Members live, the expenses they incur, their hours of work, their incomes from other sources and even their tax allowances. Comparisons were made with remuneration of roughly equivalent levels in the Civil Service.

Public attitudes were plumbed. The report tends further to alter the status of Members towards that of full-time State employees: but then the report was based upon the realities of the work done. The realities are that the situation of Members tends to make them more likely to become full-time State employees: the method of remuneration can only confirm the true situation.

Members are already full-timers. Back-benchers spend an average of sixty-three hours a week on Parliamentary work. Quite apart from further hours spent by 70 per cent of these Members on outside jobs all but one in sixteen MPs appear to be working as full-time Parliamentary workers; and work more than the forty hour week acceptable to the TUC as a normal working week. No wonder, then, that Fred Peart referred to the Boyle recommendation in terms of giving MPs the right to a rate for the job or at least a rate for the profession.

The Question of Outside Occupations

'Professionalism,' said Mr. Peart, 'in the best sense is here to stay.' Wishful thinking perhaps. Full-time does not mean professional in the sense that a job is done any better because it is the only one being done. At present only 30 per cent of Members are full-time in that they have no other job. Members were asked by the Boyle Committee whether they thought that MPs' involvement with work outside the House was beneficial or otherwise. It is interesting to note that in reply 100 per cent of present Ministers and Junior Ministers thought the involvement beneficial. Thirty per cent of back-benchers thought the involvement detrimental: an interesting figure considering that 32 per cent of back-benchers do not have any external involvement. In case anyone should think this was sour grapes, the Boyle Committee researchers broke the figure down further and it seems that only half of this 32 per cent actually thought any outside involvement to be detrimental to an MP's duties.

Among those who think that outside interests are of value to a Parliamentary career is Brian Walden. Walden believes that we have the best qualified House of Representatives in Europe.

154

He also believes that it is important to allow Members to use their existing qualifications and to acquire new ones in order to add to the general state of knowledgability of MPs.

The Boyle Committee referred to two reasons commonly given in support of the desirability of Members having outside occupations.

'1. A cross-section of Members currently involved in a wide range of part-time occupations outside the House is generally beneficial to the work of Parliament.
2. It is important to have a large number of well qualified Members to give expert scrutiny to legislation.'

In principle these are perfectly acceptable arguments for the desirability of having a diversely occupied House. Diversity is, however, not really a quality of the House of Commons. Whereas it may be true that there are a number of company directors representing the interests of a number of diverse industries, real contact with these industries is at a minimum level. Lawyers, as mentioned earlier in this book, are by far the most numerous category represented in the House and probably the most active in terms of practising their extra-Parliamentary interests. It may be argued that the understanding of the law in practise is a valuable asset to those involved in law-making. In support of this attitude are the many lawyers in the House who have never practised as such. They read for the Bar after entering the House. Barristers like Marcus Lipton, Jeremy Thorpe and Quintin Hogg who have practised only rarely, also add to the fund of legal knowledge in Parliament.

There are always dangers that outside activities of Members will endanger their impartiality. Too close an association with a group of vested interests can lead to the danger of biased behaviour. But these dangers would equally exist if Members were not allowed outside interests: there is always the risk that a Member of Parliament will be nobbled by an outside agency, whether he is allowed to have outside interests or prevented from having them.

Of the Members who do have a second occupation 19 per cent of those answering the Boyle questionnaire said that they thought such interests detrimental to the work of Parliament. The reasons for this may be purely pressure of time or they may be more related to the occasional conflict of interest which arises. In spite of the problems involved, the Members concerned would be unlikely to give up their extra-curricular activities. Their main reason for pursuing their second or third job is for the money. The inference is that these Members would not otherwise be able to live on their Parliamentary salary.

What is an MP Worth?

The size of the Parliamentary salary is another hot centre of debate. For some Members, the pre-Boyle £3,250 was more than they would have hoped to earn as teachers, secretaries, less well paid journalists, even in the lower levels of management and certainly in some of the rougher jobs like mining. For others the salary was well below the level to which they had accustomed themselves and their families previously. For many of the latter category even the more handsome post-Boyle salary of £4,500 is no compensation.

I recently spoke to one young Member of Parliament who claimed that his Parliamentary work gave him no opportunity to carry out any outside occupation. This man had had to give up his full-time job as the Managing Director of a group of companies. In consequence his gross income had fallen by £5,000 a year. This man was quite clearly suffering considerably from his change in financial status. One could not advocate that Members of Parliament be paid the same as they were earning before entering the House. The inequalities would be ludicrous. On the other hand one cannot advocate that the salary of all should equal the accustomed standards of the richest in the House in order to avoid any drop in standards for anyone.

A sensible level has to be assessed for Members' remuneration: but this is more easily said than done. Comparisons with outside professions of a roughly equal standing are not practical. What, after all, is equal standing in jobs? Judging the importance of Members of Parliament relation to other categories of manpower could be more delicate than difficult. In any case, as in every group, there are those who are more dedicated and worth more than others. Applying criteria of productivity are equally silly. Calling in management consultants might result in suggestions that Members should spend less of their sixty-three hours average working week filing through lobbies and vote by push-button instead. To carry the idea a stage further we could envisage that Members would not need to turn up at the Chamber of the House in order to make a speech. They could avoid the long boring wait while their colleagues orate, by using a system of nationwide closed circuit TV to get their point across. In fact, why bother to have a House of Parliament? The place could be demolished releasing valuable building land: Members could ask written questions of Ministers and get written replies as happens on a smaller scale now. The remainder of their valuable time could be devoted to thoroughly servicing their constituents and carrying out valuable research into new methods of Government.

So much for the productivity concept. The work of the House is not measurable, either in terms of the number of constituents' grievances redressed, the number of Bills passed, clauses voted upon or committees advised. Spurious, then, is any attempt to compare the work of MPs with, say, doctors or managers.

Neither is the value of Members easily judged by public opinion. The Boyle Committee did, however, ask a sample of 2,020 people what they thought about the earnings of various professional groups. Significantly more people thought MPs to be underpaid after learning the true conditions of payment than thought so before. In fact many people thought Members were earning more than they were. Although 682 of the sample thought MPs gross salaries exceeded £4,000 p.a., it is interesting to note that 37 per cent of these thought they were being paid about the right amount. On the other hand, 389 respondents thought Members earned gross salaries of under

£3,000 and of these 20 per cent thought Members were overpaid. The same thing happens every time groups of workers strike. It is all relative.

Of all respondents, before they learned the true salary and conditions, 12 per cent thought MPs grossly overpaid. After being told that on average Members earned £3,500 plus £500 allowance towards a secretary and probably paid £1,000 of their income out in doing their job, only 4 per cent thought they were grossly overpaid.

The analysis of public attitudes towards the payment of their MPs would probably reveal a great deal of misunderstanding about the job and its importance. Compared with the attitudes expressed in the Boyle survey for other professional groups, MPs came out only fairly well. It is interesting to note that whereas only one per cent of the sample thought their GP grossly overpaid and 4 per cent thought him grossly underpaid, solicitors were considered grossly overpaid by 14 per cent of the sample and grossly underpaid by less than half a per cent. Sympathy for teachers was closer to that expressed for doctors, but junior hospital doctors were considered grossly underpaid by 29 per cent of the sample. MPs might worry slightly at being put so near to solicitors in the initial assessment. (Only one per cent thought MPs grossly underpaid.) 37 per cent and 25 per cent respectively thought solicitors and MPs rather overpaid as to only 7 and 6 per cent holding that view about doctors and teachers.

Clearly, publicity given to doctors, junior hospital doctors and teachers pay and overwork has had a softening effect on public opinion about their levels of remuneration. Ten years ago people probably considered their doctors rather comfortably off. Lately they are regarded as being underpaid and overworked. Since solicitors are in a position to charge fat fees for what sometimes seems to be negligible effort they should hardly be expected to receive much sympathy.

Members of Parliament should perhaps be perturbed that public opinion of their worth corresponds with that of solicitors.

Referring to the information obtained in the Boyle public

attitude survey, the late Sir Harry Legge Bourke said: 'When one realises the misconceptions that exists in the public mind about our salaries, remuneration, pensions, and so on, one realises that however desirable it may be to leave this to be decided by public opinion poll, one cannot do that if one expects to get a sensible or just solution.'

Justice and common sense are the most important factors in establishing the remuneration rate of Members. Establishing the basic salary may be one problem, but it cannot be considered in isolation from the working expenses that a Member incurs by virtue of his responsibilities. The practical aspects of the business are that a Member should be paid a salary and allowances which enable him to live at a standard enjoyed by an average member of society at that time, and to cope with the extra expense in which his position undoubtedly involves him. That the sum arrived at should not take additional income into account, has been the verdict of both the Lawrence and Boyle Committees. Boyle reported: 'The Committee preferred not to express an opinion on this but took into account that fact that the House of Commons contained and was likely to continue to contain a number of Members who did not have the opportunity of supplementing their salary by earnings outside the House: and, secondly, that the possibility of making those earnings varied from Member to Member.'

How Much 'Extra' Do Members Really Make?

About one-third of the Members in the present House have no extra source of income. Extra earnings for the two-thirds that do, vary from less than £200 to over £5,000.

Two of the Members I spoke to, one Labour and one Conservative, said that their total income exceeded £15,000 a year. Neither were office holders or had been in the past. One of these told me that he had suffered considerable reduction in income from his business through coming to Parliament. Boyle reported that 20 per cent of Members of Parliament, among the 70 per cent making outside earnings, were making more than £5,000 a year extra. Nearly one-third of those with an outside income were, however, making only between one and three thousand a year extra. A further 19 per cent make less than £500 a year extra, and more than half of these make less than £250. A fairly substantial number (17 per cent) were making between three and five thousand a year.

This way one can say that more than one-quarter of the entire House arc making at least an extra three thousand a year and a further quarter are making at least one thousand a year extra. From this one can see that about half the Members of Parliament are almost entirely dependent on their Parliamentary salary and expenses to see them through.

Members of Parliament are widely suspected of making fortunes out of their position. Some Members clearly do make use of the exceptional opportunities which exist: the brighter Member is well placed to use skills and specialist knowledge in consultancies; is far better placed for offers of advisory positions than is a mineworker or a lorry driver.

On the other hand, the pressures of Parliamentary work are increasing. A man already working a sixty-three-hour week has not so much time available for outside activities as one working the comfortable thirty or so hours that pre-war Members were accustomed to. The offers of jobs would also seem to be less freely available than in the past. As Jerry Wiggin said in the House: 'There seems to be the view, held by a number of people that it is easy for Members to obtain part-time work outside this place. It is far from easy. The days of the non-executive directorships which can be picked up by Members of Parliament because of the letters at the end of their names are past. Regular executive work is hard to find because it upsets other members of a firm who are in regular employment when, at two-o'clock a Member says: "I must now go off for Question Time".'

Mr. Wiggin may be right: certainly a number of the newer Conservative intake of 1970 seems to have been disappointed by the lack of offers coming their way. This may be an indication of some reduction in the status of MPs. It may be that the newer Members, Mr. Wiggin included, do not have the sort of qualification that companies are looking for: in all things the

MP with good connections is more likely to find himself on a company's notepaper than one without.

Ministers are more popular for directorships than ordinary Members for the double reason that they have more inside knowledge as well as more status. Similarly, Conservatives get more offers than Labour men because more of them have business experience.

Membership of Parliament may carry fewer sinecures in the outside world than is commonly assumed: but if the opportunities to work for existing companies are disappointing, there are unlimited opportunities for the entrepreneur. Most Members in the £10,000-plus bracket are probably involved in other forms of self-employed activity. This is the real advantage to Members of being self-employed and of being able to adapt the hours of Parliamentary work. Solicitors, barristers and journalists can easily bend their Parliamentary hours to suit their other work. Unless they have a Committee to sit on, the mornings are free: it is possible to get a pair on other occasions, although the number of three-line Whips is increasing. The growing number of Members who are founder partners in advertising agencies, public relations consultancies, air charter organisations and publishing houses is growing.

Members of Parliament may try to sound hard done by but a number of them have some thriving interests. The entrepreneurial attitude is important if a Member is to make a good living without too much corruption. The attitude of the employed man is less likely to move him into the big time: and sitting around hoping for consultancies is not guaranteed to bring the bigger prizes in, even for a Member of Parliament.

Not all Members have either the ability or the attitude required for making extra money: acquiring consultancies or directorships, or setting up slick agency operations are not activities which come naturally to a man who has been a carpenter, a tool-cutter or a boilermaker for the first twenty years of his working life. Many Labour Members come into this category. They are working class men without the natural smoothness of their middle class colleagues. These sort of men are cut off from the fruits of business connections: like the growing number of lecturers, teachers, and many administrators, they are neither qualified for or inclined towards the entrepreneurial world. These types of men form the 50 per cent of the House of Commons which is virtually completely dependent on the Parliamentary salary for their maintenance in the job.

Assessment of the salaries must therefore be on the assumption of exclusive and full-time employment. 'The rate for the job' is now settled at a middle managerial level — though, as Boyle says, 'This is not permanently pegged. It would be wrong, that it should be adjusted automatically in relation to the cost of living or wage and salary indices.' Boyle's attitude was that, on the one hand, this would give MPs an unfair advantage over the public; secondly, and more importantly 'the job needs to be revalued from time to time in the light of new circumstances'.

The Expenses Factor

To the man in the street £4,500 a year looks like a reasonable salary; £3,250 looked good to about half of Lord Boyle's sample of public. The fact that the Member of Parliament incurs considerable expense in doing his duty is usually overlooked. In fact, the salary of £3,250 was broken down into £2,000 salary and £1,200 Parliamentary or 'taxable expense allowance'. An additional £500 allowance towards secretarial services was added together with some free postage and telephone facilities in 1970. In addition, the Member was getting free travel (first class) between London and his constituency. The theory behind this system of remuneration is that those who could afford it provide themselves with proper services, and the Parliamentary salary and allowances would keep the poor men with their heads just above the water-level.

The situation inproved in December 1971 when, after the recommendations of the Boyle Committee had been debated, the following was resolved by the House:

> *Salary:* £4,500 (Excepting Ministers and other paid office holders who get Parliamentary salary of £3,000 plus their Ministerial salary.)

Expenses: Supplementary London allowance of £175 per annum for those living in London.

£750 to help maintain accommodation in London for those living elsewhere.

£1,375 for secretarial assistance and expenses until March 1973 and £1,000 from March 1973.

Travel within constituencies.

Travel between constituency and London.

Ten free travel vouchers a year for wives.

In the debate on the second reading of the Bill, Jerry Wiggin said: 'Since I first came to the House, not very long ago*, there have been substantial improvements in many of our allowances. They were sorely needed because even in my first year only three years ago I found that my salary after expenses did not exceed £1,000!' I do not consider,' went on Mr. Wiggin, 'that anyone can consider that to be adequate remuneration for our responsibilities and the work we have to do.' Earlier in the same debate Charles Pannell had said: 'No one could say that I came to the House for the money at the end of it.'

Members of Parliament will undoubtedly find their circumstances improved by the new Salaries Bill. The question of whether the problem has been dealt with correctly, however, is still wide open.

The decision has been taken to separate the financial demands of the job as much as possible from remuneration for the work put in. For instance, the fact that the average MP spends £800 a year maintaining some kind of accommodation in London apart from his home, is dealt with by providing a £750 allowance for that purpose. Designed to cover four nights a week for thirty-four weeks, this is a reasonable contribution to the undoubted expense of maintaining two homes. Boyle expresses the opinion that this particular form of expense was the biggest single item for the Member to cover. Other expenses, such as the cost of keeping a wife dressed for the role she has to play, keeping up certain standards in the home, paying for research work, entertaining constituents,

* March 1969 — Weston-super-Mare by-election.

travel abroad or in the UK are not even allowable for tax.

Secretarial expenses are another major item. A good full-time secretary costs at least £2,000 a year, London rate. From the Boyle questionnaire it emerged that only 30 per cent of Members employed a secretary for more than thirty hours a week. This does not indicate a lack of need for a secretary so much as the inability to afford one. It is a fair bet that most of those employing a secretary full time are either office holders (only 3 per cent according to Boyle were not employing a secretary at all) or else the Members who are making at least three thousand on top of their MP's salary, outside the House.

That services of this kind are badly needed is evidenced by the fact that a number of MPs simply do not bother to answer letters. Having written to several myself, I know of at least six who clearly do not even open letters. The secretarial servicing of Members who cannot afford or who do not need a full-time secretary is done through 'pool facilities'. This in effect is an outside typing agency whose main disadvantage, according to Ben Whittaker, is that the rate of return of letters was abysmally slow.

Secretarial services are not the only commodity in short supply at the House. There are only 172 single rooms, 49 double rooms, 11 treble rooms and 29 spare desks available for 630 Members. Talk of a new Parliament building has been circulating for years and tends to cause laughter when mentioned. This perhaps is the kind of facility which more than any other is genuinely required to make Parliament more efficient — if not more effective. Of the school of thought that thinks all the ills of Parliament can be cured by a new building is Ben Whittaker. He belongs to the group that look towards the American Congressman's style of Government with longing eyes.

The idea that MPs should be provided with at least one office, a secretary and possibly an assistant too is becoming more fashionable. The pressure of work is tending to increase; legislation flows faster and consequently the amount of sheer reading that a Member has to do limits the available time for other activities. Secretaries can cut down on time-wasting telephone calls; and whereas a typing pool can only work from a tape a good secretary can devise her own replies to letters. Moreover, opening and reading one hundred letters a week can take up much of a Member's time. All good management depends on there being someone to delegate to. Members of Parliament only cope with so much without that facility.

The disagreement among Members about the new trend towards State-financed services is largely one between the new men and the old. Enoch Powell, a man whose understanding of the twentieth century is not as clear as his grasp of the eighteenth and nineteenth, is very much opposed to the trend towards State-employed MPs. The view is tenable but contrary to all visible signs of desirable change.

The decision to separate several different categories of incurred expense from the ordinary salary is a very firm step towards State employee status. 'Reimbursement,' says Mr. Powell with disgust, 'is the mark of the employee.' He is right. The argument about whether it is desirable or not that Members of Parliament should become employees is very much weighted by its association with efficiency factors. Powell also says: 'Until very recently it was the discretion of an honourable Member — for some purposes we are still treated, as I believe we should be in every sense, as self-employed. It was his judgment, it was a matter between himself and his constituents, it was a matter on which he formed his own judgment as to the way in which he could best do his duty and contribute to this House.'

The more reimbursed expenses a Member accepts, according to Powell, the less he can operate on his own discretion and the more he is controlled as to the duties he should carry out. This is all absolutely right. The trouble is the very difficulties expressed by Members trying to survive and cope with their expenses as self-employed men, indicate the need for a very much higher salary than any currently recommended.

Boyle, in fact, did say that the £3,250 of 1964 could be considered to be equivalent to £5,500 in 1972. His committee chose to recommend a smaller salary which, when the allowances are thrown in, adds up to about the same. The whole basis of the Boyle Commission was to discover which areas of the country, what basis of living and what kind of tax position required the most assistance. A smaller salary and larger and more variable allowances are therefore a more just way of dealing with these basic inequalities.

But is this enough? Members of Parliament in Britain are shoe-string representatives compared with many other comparable countries. Canada, for instance, a country with a Westminister model system and with a cost of living only marginally different from Britain, pays her Members of Parliament twenty thousand dollars a year and provides them with a full-time secretary and research assistance. Constituents write fewer letters to their Members, finding it easier to use the free phone-in service to their Member's office instead.

Perhaps Members of Parliament in Britain should be paid between eight and ten thousand pounds a year and provided with similar services. Of course there is the danger that the more services provided the lazier or else the more occupied with their own financial interests the Members would become.

But then such a salary and assistance level would enable firmer control on Members' extra-curricular financial interests. Perhaps these should be disallowed altogether? There is also the problem that there are some Members already, who abuse the tax-payers stipend, using it more as a club subscription than a means to help do their duty by their constituents. Another alternative is for the constituents to vote their Member a salary every year, for if anyone knows the value of an MP, it is his own constituents.

If there are Members who spend all day in the House but never leave the Strangers bar; if there are Members who pocket their salary and ignore both Parliament and their constituency affairs, there are also a greater number who are dutiful and responsible and deserve a fair opportunity to do their work under reasonable conditions. A little more expense on the machinery of representation would not necessarily mean paying Members large salaries, which would then enable them to become divorced from the financial struggles of the majority of their constituents. But desk space, secretaries and adequate research assistance are fundamentals long overdue. That these must be provided by the State, that most Members could not be expected to afford London office space and the wages of two full-time helpers should now be obvious.

The level of assistance actually required by Members has as yet to be established. By way of an experiment recently, the Rowntree Trust offered six research assistants to Members of Parliament. Two were to be allocated to each party.

Since the Boyle recommendations, a Member of Parliament is allowed a grant of £300 a year towards employing a research assistant. 'No one,' said Joel Barnett in the Salaries Bill debate, 'imagines that the services of a qualified research assistant could be obtained for £300 a year.' Mr. Barnett went on to say that it was unlikely that any Member would need such assistants full time but that a shared assistant being paid about £2,000 a year could service three MPs. Tax relief was what Mr. Barnett was after in the same way as he was looking for tax relief on funds spent to take himself abroad.

The new Bill makes provision for a fund from which a Member should be able to claim a grant for necessary foreign travel. If a Member wishes to make his mind up about an issue before voting on it, and needs to travel abroad before coming to a reasonably informed conclusion he should do so, according to Mr. Barnett. 'If this sort of travel is not to be paid for out of reimbursable expenses,' he says, 'it should be deductible for tax.'

At the other end of the extreme on this issue is Andrew Faulds, whose opinion of the grant is that it will enable Members to take holidays on pretext of Parliamentary business. 'I, as Opposition Spokesman for the arts,' said Faulds in the Boyle debate, 'can choose if I so wish to go on a happy, sunny holiday to Egypt to check up whether the Egyptian authorities have been kind enough and good enough to give us enough of the Tutankhamen treasure to exhibit next March at the British Museum.'

Andrew Faulds well knew when he made that speech that there are many Members who spend a large proportion of their time, angling for, negotiating about and going on dubious foreign expeditions. Joel Barnett, however, had the right answer. If such trips were tax deductible Members would not be compromising themselves so often for these jaunts — so often to the scenes of *coups d'etats* and at the bidding of unsavoury dictatorships. Travel abroad to these situations is, of course, necessary for groups of MPs. That is why it is so important that they should be self or British Government financed and therefore independent of the smell of inevitable corruption.

'If Members were paid enough,' says Brian Walden, 'there would not be so many of them grubbing around for these trips.'

Old Age and Rainy Days

Pensions are yet another matter. One of the more unfair aspects of life in Parliament is that, whatever other white collar work one might have been doing, one would probably have been entitled to a reasonable pension on retirement. A spell as an MP fairly cuts into anyone's pension rights. It is only fair therefore that MPs should have some sort of pension when they retire. The self-employed MP should naturally be expected to make his own pension arrangements. Private pensions schemes are now proliferating. On the other hand, service men and civil servants receive pensions, so why, since they are semi-employed anyway, should MPs not get the same treatment?

In fact there has been a pension scheme for MPs since 1965. At this time an Exchequer fund of £100,000 was established. Members paid £150 per annum, and after ten years were entitled to £600 a year after the age of 65. Only slightly more generous was the pension of £900 per annum awarded after fifteen years' service, with the prospect of a further £24 per year for every additional year's service. On the other hand, the final value of this scheme sounds fair in comparison to many other pension arrangements. It allows for a pension of 60 per cent of salary after forty-five years' service.

Boyle reviewed the situation in a practical fashion. Ten

years' service, he reported, could well in fact represent the life of three Parliaments and represent as much as twelve years' service. Similarly, he went on, 'Five years' service could require service in two Parliaments and probably represent about eight years' service in practice.' Since the life of Parliament is four years on average, Boyle recommended that the qualifying period for a pension should be four years.

Additional recommendations were that the reckonable service could only fairly be assessed in days, as opposed to completed years which, said Boyle, 'Could deprive a Member of credit for many months of service. Sixty-five was,' said Boyle, 'too late a retiring age', considering the wear and tear of political life on Members. He recommended retirement at sixty instead. The long list of Prospective Conservative candidates waiting for constituencies must have heaved a sigh of gratitude at that one.

The amount of pension payable is limited by Inland Revenue rules to two-thirds of the final salary. This is what MPs will now get, with a built-in provision to 'maintain the value of pensions against future rises in the cost of living, as in the case of other public service pensioners'. Members will in future be expected to pay three-eighths of the total cost of the scheme, i.e. 5 per cent of their salary.

One of the snags with paying pensions to MPs has always been the sporadic nature of the service. MPs come and go, and may return to the House after a period of absence two or even three times. The new Boyle recommendations cater for this peculiarity. MPs can now be safely said to be well looked after. Indeed with the exception of the Members who are totally dependent on their Parliamentary salary and therefore their Parliamentary pension (it is unlikely that a man earning £4,000 a year could afford more than one set of contributions), MPs are now in a reasonably secure position financially: and in a better one than other public service pensioners who retire on half pay.

Security of tenure in the job is not necessarily so certain. In the past there have been cases of hardship among Members who have lost their seats. As recently as 1970, there were a number of dire cases. Members in jobs, like teaching and lecturing, who lost their seats in the June Election were also too late to get themselves posts for the following year. Most teaching posts are filled by the preceding Easter, and this means that anyone who is not fixed up then is out of work for nearly eighteen months. As some form of safeguard against such situations the Boyle Committee recommended the introduction of a Henry VIII sounding 'severance pay'. Members who lose their seats will now continue to receive their Parliamentary salary for three months.

In debate on the Boyle Report, Members were critical of severance arrangements and even of the proposal to pay Members during the election period. James Wellbeloved was severe when he said: 'I see no justification for one candidate in each of the 630 constituencies being in the privileged position of being paid his full-time salary during the campaign.' Wellbeloved recognised that people working for some large firms or privately wealthy candidates were in this favoured position already. So indeed are Ministers who get their salary while fighting the election. But Wellbeloved went on: 'Whether he is a Communist, Liberal or anything else, he may be losing wages as a carpenter, a plumber or a dock worker and there can be no justification for saying that ex-Members of Parliament should be paid during a General Election campaign.'

The arguments about Members' pay will never be entirely settled. Circumstances of Members are continually changing. The nature of the work, its importance, its duration, and the expense incurred during its course, all affect the assessment of the rate of the job. There is no perfect assessment: and while the arguments swing from one extreme to the other, the safest place can only be somewhere in between.

No one should suffer unduly from being an MP. No Member's wife should have to work to support her family. No Member should be put into the position whereby he has to take outside work against his wishes, or where he is put in danger of compromising his political position for financial gain. On the other hand, there is a valid argument for dividing expenses of doing the job from the stipend needed for personal survival.

Some Members will spend more than others on their work. In the past even travel within a constituency had to be paid for by the Member. Now this is not the case. The arguments over foreign travel have also reached the stage where most MPs accept that the Exchequer should give some help.

A £20,000 fund is now in existence. In spite of the disapproval of Andrew Faulds, the fund will give grants to Members for necessary travel abroad. Tam Dalyell questioned 'Whether this is a realistic starting figure'. After Ministers 'Have had their wallop,' he went on, 'what will be left for the rest of us?' One alternative suggested was that the sums spent on foreign travel should be tax deductible: the danger of jaunting at public expense would not be so great if this were so. Another problem associated with a central fund is that of awarding grants for trips. As Arthur Lewis sarcastically remarked: 'It is the usual crowd who go to NATO, the Council of Europe, WEU, IPU and CPA, and then they occasionally turn up here to show that they are Members.' He said: 'I would feel much happier if he (the Leader of the House) did it than if it were left to the usual channels.' By 'usual channels' Lewis was referring to the Whips' recommendation that goes to the Speaker, who 'decides' on the beneficiaries.

Somehow Members seem fairly well off. Compared with the situation of the early sixties, when to quote Norman Atkinson, 'Some Members suffered such great poverty on their £1,750 that they could not afford any lodgings and had to sleep on the benches in the House', things are extremely comfortable. Ministers are even better off, although not with the universal approval. James Wellbeloved asked the House: 'Are we to award the Secretary of State for Education and Science (then Margaret Thatcher) with an extra £129 a week for snatching away school children's milk?' Better, perhaps, than risk the dangers of corruption.

There will always be many points of view. But the last word surely must go to Ernle Money, Member of Ipswich, who said during the course of the 1971 salaries Bill reading: 'Probably the worst form of corruption is worry about money.' He went on to remind the House that Burke was constantly in trouble with his bank manager and 'that his career was ruined in consequence'. He went on: 'There is nothing more debilitating to Hon. Members than to be servants of their bank managers rather than servants of the public.' The public can rest easy for the time being, at least, in the knowledge that their servants are adequately, though not excessively, paid and that their welfare is at least as well catered for as that of most employees.

2

A BRIBE BY
ANY OTHER NAME

If Members of Parliament are valued at the level of lower grade management or of small-time professionals in terms of their legislative functions, there are other interests which are prepared to put a higher price on their heads. Parliament may not offer much in the way of power, or even money to its Members. Its power may seem small compared with that of multi-million pound international companies: its influence small compared with that of television, the Church or the City. But in a society which accepts as basic the Rule of Law, Parliament as Law Maker is supreme. So much so that the very interests which seem to dwarf Parliament, MPs and the Government by their power, have to seek favours through Parliament itself to achieve what they want.

Individual Members of Parliament have a limited influence. But they have influence in Parliament as critics and in Government as decision-makers. While Law is supreme, Parliament is important and what passes there can influence the profits of companies, the power of institutions, the fortunes of the nation and the lives of individuals. Anyone who wants anything lawfully must first look to Parliament. Seldom wonder then that Members of Parliament are wooed and lobbied, sought after and employed to represent all manner of interests over and above those of their constituents.

As Machiavelli so rightly pointed out: 'The people are everywhere anxious not to be dominated and oppressed by the nobles and the nobles are out to dominate and oppress the people.' Times have not changed. But for nobles now read vested interests. Parliament has stood between them — these two 'opposed ambitions' since it began and no doubt saved us from bloody revolution. But while Parliament exists to represent the people, vested interests are not without their stake.

Members are always on the look-out for extra money. If it can be earned honestly so much the better. It is a general assumption that politicians are crooked — and in it for what they can get. But self-interest is no more absent in politicians than in other people and the opportunity to earn extra money is not normally turned down by anyone.

For Members of Parliament self-interest is one of a number of priorities which also includes the interests of constituents, the interest of party, the interests of family. It is the order in which they place these priorities that must give rise to concern. MPs are bound to place commercial interest somewhere in amongst this order of priorities. The crucial question is where? When a Member receives payments, however honourably earned, from an outside source — to what extent has his order of priorites suffered distortion? To what extent are Members tied to the interests, who pays them, and how much are the course of true politics perverted by the money bags of sordid commerce or the pull of unorthodox political activities?

The Built-in Vested Interests

To a certain extent all Members of the two main political parties in the House are committed to a vested interest by their membership of their Party. The Conservatives represent the might of capitalism, and the account books of the Conservative Party and many big companies bears that out: the Labour Party is financially supported by the Trades Unions and is committed to their interest to that degree. It could be argued that accepting money is not necessarily a commitment to support: but that commitment is only registered in that when policies change, so do the sources of cash.

Money is very powerful: and Members of Parliament are not ignorant of its lure. Most Members (see previous Chapter) accept some financial support. Even Labour Members, whom I have heard protesting innocence of outside interests as evidence of their dedication as full-time MPs, are among those accepting financial support from Trades Unions. The support given by sponsoring Unions is often more in kind than in cash. The Union will contribute 80 per cent of the election expenditure, sometimes 100 per cent and 60–65 per cent of the agent's salary. The normal running costs of the local party offices can be paid for by the Union; and a contribution made towards the MPs expenses. Unions have, in the past, paid their MPs a retainer; this might be as little as a hundred pounds. Nevertheless this kind of support can be very helpful to a poor man, and noticeable by its absence if it is withdrawn. Union sponsorship certainly commands loyalty, whether related to financial support or not. Union Members have been known to act together with their colleagues to put pressure on party leadership.

According to the Union's General Secretary, Ernest Roberts, the AUEW Group in the House of Commons acted together successfully over a London Transport Underground issue. According to Norman Atkinson, one of the AUEW-sponsored MPs, this happens rarely. 'I'm ahead of you there,' he told me suspiciously. 'The Union does not affect the way we vote.' The Union Group meets, however, with its Union Executive every three months and runs through a joint agenda. If there is an issue which the Union feels is going against its interests, the MPs will be asked to put pressure on the Parliamentary Party and the leadership. There is no compulsion. Ernest Roberts says: 'MPs vote as to whether to raise the issue with the PLP or else directly in the House.'

There is no doubt that Union-sponsored Members act in support of their Union on occasion. During the miners' strike in February 1972, Roy Mason, a former Minister of Power, and four other Parliamentary members of the National Union of Mineworkers joined a picket group outside the Battersea Power Station. In a television interview Mason said: 'This is a gesture of solidarity by the card-carrying Members of the House of Commons Branch of the Union of Mineworkers.' Of their own free will there is no reason why anyone should not join a miners' picket line. The question is whether the threat to take away sponsorship is ever made if a Member repeatedly goes against the policy of the Union.

In 1955 rumours circulated to the effect that Aneurin Bevan would lose the support of the National Union of Mineworkers' £150 allowance for his rebellion over the nuclear deterrent issue. Bevan invoked Privilege on the principle that the Report of the Committee of Privileges had stated: 'It is a breach of privilege to take or threaten action which is not merely calculated to affect the Members' course of action in Parliament but is of a kind against which it is absolutely necessary that Members should be protected if they are to discharge their duties as such independently without fear of punishment or reward.'

Clearly Privilege is breached every day by the threats of Whips and constituency parties to withdraw their support from erring Members. More sinister, however, than any of these influences, is the fact that compulsion or threats are not normally used. The Members are well aware on which side their bread is buttered and act accordingly. The Conservative habit of giving knighthoods is similarly a bribe which does not always work. If honours are intended to shut up troublesome right-wingers they sometimes fail; and they lack the advantages of Union sponsorship in that they cannot be revoked. But the existence of a carrot of some kind has an effect on Members' behaviour. Whoever pays MPs money has some measure of power over their responses. The extent of that power will depend on three things: the integrity of the MP, his need for money and the size of the consideration.

Declared and Undeclared Interests

More insidious than any general application of a blanket vested interest are the private interests which Members develop of their own accord. These are just as likely to breach Privilege but the breach is less likely to be made known.

As already stated, two-thirds of Members have alternative

occupations. Some of their own making: others, a result of specialist knowledge are forms of employment by outside concerns. These occupations may not imply more of an obligation than Union sponsorship does to influence the work of the House. Nor are they likely to bring in any more money.

The price put on a Member will vary according to his position and his access to information; to his own special skills and the degree of his influence. If it is true that every man has his price, it is also true that each man has his cash value. Ministers have more value than other office holders. These latter more than ordinary back-benchers; and some back-benchers more than others. Likewise different 'jobs' will have a different price-tag according to what is required of them.

Not all of the MPs on retainers and directorships, salaries and fees from outside bodies are employed for the same reason. A minority are, however, deliberately employed for the two-way assistance they can give to a commercial lobby. On the one hand the Member acts as a consultant, advising the outside interest on the political position regarding its plans. There are dangers that Members could release confidential information gained at specialist committees; or, if as so often, the Member is a Minister, give the benefit of detailed knowledge on some special project. The Member in doing this will not usually exceed his discretion. Even so, there are occasions when this must have occurred. The Member will know how little he has to impart to keep his retainer flowing, and keep his disclosures to a minimum. He will also know how much he can get away with and still retain a veneer of integrity. This is not a question of giving away the blueprints; more of reading out the odd formula from time to time.

The other half of the bargain is for the Member of Parliament the most difficult. When the opportunity occurs for the commercial interest to make a move, it may be necessary for the Member to do some gentle lobbying, or even ask a question in the House. Clearly it is to the Member's advantage if the interests he represents are undeclared. When a Member has known commercial interests he is suspect. John Gorst's position over Commercial Radio, was exactly this. He told me: 'I have to be extremely careful. I cannot be seen to be actively lobbying.'

Before John Gorst became a Member of Parliament he had three Members working for him in the House. Mr. Gorst cannot actively lobby for the interests he represents, but he is in an ideal position to pick out other people who can do the job for him.

Should any Member of Parliament want to lobby by proxy he has a head start at least on outside concerns. That Gorst should be anxious to keep his lobbying secret is not surprising. Most lobbyists are far from anxious to have their existence widely known. The association of a Member of Parliament with some commercial lobby may be perfectly innocent and within the bounds of his Parliamentary integrity. But if it is not, who is to know the difference?

After growing parliamentary pressure MPs voted 363–168 in favour of an official register of interests on May 22nd, 1974. The Liberal Party has for some time had a list available in its Whips office of the interests of its MPs. The party has more than once been vocal in the cause of declared interests. Yet it would be possible for any one Liberal MP to have interests about which his colleagues know nothing and which he did not declare.

Andrew Roth who is the author of a useful book — *The Business Background of MPs*, has himself admitted that his sources of information are not all encompassing. Directorships are fairly easily discovered. Items such as incomes from journalism or the professions are usually quite happily declared. But as Roth says: 'If they want to keep things secret they will.'

William Hamilton, the indefatigable Member for West Fife, said as much in the House on March 10th, 1967. Begging leave to introduce a Bill to provide for the establishment of a register of interests he said: 'Most Members seem quite pre-prepared to disclose what those interests are but at the moment it is entirely voluntary.' He also referred to one Member who had 'not listed his activities in *Who's Who* nor declared his interest in certain companies to the House of Commons nor volunteered the information to Mr. Roth for inclusion in his succession of books on Members' business interests.'

It is the backhanders, the mysterious retainers, the secret gifts, the payments in kind, the fees and the honoraria that go unlisted. And well they might. But if they are nowhere published and nowhere registered, who, even in the full knowledge of their existence can make public a Member's association with any concern. Corruption is hard enough to prove where it exists. What can a nebulous series of payments show without considerably detailed knowledge of what was done in return?

Corruption is too strong a word to apply to a situation in which no active decision-making is involved. Yet influence can be corrupting according to the way in which it is used. Members of Parliament are widely regarded as corrupt, and indeed in a minor way they are. None of them are prepared to recognise the possible corrupt motives of their colleagues; perhaps because they operate only on one issue part of the time, and go straight during the remainder. Typical of the attitude of MPs to whom I have spoken on this subject is this statement by Charles Pannell in a speech made during the debate on the Boyle Report:

'I do not regard the House as a corrupt place. I refused to serve on the Select Committee on Members interests because I thought that it cast an undeserved shadow and an imputation that the House did not deserve. I believe that Members can be found out in this place and that they can declare their interests.'

But Pannell went on to say, 'If they do not declare them it is pretty grim at the end of the day.'

Members in general do not know what the interests of other Members are and there is no way anyone can find out — short of deliberate investigation. But even that does not reveal much.

Members of Parliament have the starriest eyes of any when it comes to their own position in life. They have a far greater impression of their own importance and of their own powers than anyone else; and this extends to their conception of their own purity of motive. It is very likely that, as Peter Kirk and other Members said to me, 'There is far more corruption in Local Government than there is in Central Government.' The implication of the remark is that Members of Parliament have more integrity on the whole than local councillors. On my experience I would say that this is true; on the other hand the corruption is on quite another level.

The Suspicion of Corrupt Practices

A comparison between Ministerial corruption and local authority corruption is more relevant. Real corruption shows up more in a situation where contracts are to be awarded; and the paw-greasing that goes on in local Government to this effect is a well known art of getting business. Decisions in Central Government on contracts are often policy decisions. When a contract was awarded for expensive low-altitude flying radar equipment in British Hunter fighters, it was awarded to a company whose links with France were appropriate to our other aviation interests in that country, rather than to an American Company who had a more advanced product, but less of a political case.

The field of defence and aviation do offer opportunities for skulduggery on a large scale, though not always by politicians.

In April 1964 a report from the Comptroller and Auditor General to Parliament brought to light the fact that Ferranti had made a profit of 72 per cent on a Ministry of Defence contract. The contract, for Bloodhound Mark I missiles had been arranged in 1960 with the then Ministry of Aviation, under Julian Amery. On a total agreed price of just over £12 millions Ferranti had somehow contrived to make a profit of £5,772,964.

The Ministry pleaded ignorance: that it had been taken advantage of by Ferranti, but in reply Ferranti said: 'It is not true. So far from being ignorant of the facts, the Ministry of Aviation had in their possession before prices were settled, the company's actual production costs of the production of Bloodhound I.'

The Public Accounts Committee weakly held out that it was

the duty of the company to remind the Ministry of the original production costs before agreeing the delivery price. Clearly there was either incompetence of an unprecedented dimension or else someone on one side or other had been on the fiddle. An inquiry was instituted. While it sat, leaks of information flowed fast and furious to the press; so much so that the Opposition complained in Parliament that Julian Amery was responsible for them. Eventually the inquiry reported to the House.

In the meantime Ferranti had offered to refund £4½ millions of the 'excessive profit' and the offer was duly accepted. The report put most of the blame on to the accounting system used by Ferranti. Saying: 'The firm does not record its costs in a way that enables a reasonable assessment of actual costs per contract to be made.'

The Ministry was criticised for a 'lack of direction and drive to make the most of the Ministry's resources': a slap for Mr. Amery.

The report was accepted and the fuss died down. There was no evidence of corruption for the Opposition to feed upon. This was a case of incompetence of unbelievable proportion. The original suspicion that something more sinister had occurred may have been a flashback to the Marconi scandal in which 'Ministers were actively and corruptly involved' — as Peter Kirk says: 'The Marconi case was hushed up. Most of the people involved were in a majority on the inquiry.'

Major public scandal can cause a Government to fall from office, and most cases of Central Government incompetence and corruption are given the blind eye treatment. Even a man of conscience will be prevented from blowing a corruption story about a Member of his own party precisely because of this: and the number of effective hush-ups probably depend very much on the effectiveness of this factor. The Profumo affair would almost certainly have been hushed up had the Opposition not been the prime movers. And there are at least a dozen potential Profumo scandals in every Government.

As Peter Kirk says: 'The things that catch Governments out are not the political things and therefore it is up to the Government to know what is going on and to inactivate scandal.'

Scandal is obviously more explosive where Ministers rather than ordinary back-benchers are involved. A man's enemies, or critics are keen enough to exploit his difficulties. An example is the way in which Reginald Maudling's association with international financier Hoffman has been held up to the limelight by *Private Eye*. According to Kirk, Maudling's connection with Hoffman 'is just bad luck. It could happen,' he adds charitably, 'to anyone.' And as the recent Poulson disclosures have shown — it happens to Reggie Maudling relatively often.

Mr. Maudling's bad luck in these matters is an unfortunate feature. Once regarded as one of the finest financial brains in the country, Maudling has an uncanny knack of picking up bum directorships. In the words of a city man, 'he has been mixed up with some very funny people financially'. IOS was another of Maudling's risky associations. Bad luck may also have accounted for Richard Reader Harris's implication in the Rolls Razor Affair. The jury acquitted Harris. He had had an unfortunate association. The fact remains while the luck holds out these relationships can be very profitable.

Suspicion of guilt by association is unfair but inevitable. Certainly, the fact that a man is associated with a company later found to have had fraudulent dealings does not suggest that he is himself corrupt: nor does it suggest that he will pull political strings to help the company concerned whether before or after it runs into difficulties.

As William Hamilton has pointed out, the Members associated with the crashed companies of Savundra and Bloom 'may have been innocent dupes used by companies engaged in rather dubious business practices which felt that the association of Hon. Members' names with their activities might help to create an aura of respectability and honesty sufficiently convincing to gull the public.'

It is well known that new companies usually make a fairly careful selection of names most suited to their operations. A respectable list of names on the notepaper is well worth a few thousand a year to a company setting out for the big time. Members of Parliament could well be gullible. They could also be greedy. The number of directorships and consultancies floating around is reasonably limited. Not all Members will be sufficiently well known or respected. Thus the bigger the ambitions of the enterprise the bigger the names it must buy.

Reginald Maudling had the advantage of being both a big name and an ex-Chancellor of the Exchequer. He was capable of contributing both respectability and inside information to any enterprise with which he became associated. After his defeat in the party leadership elections he could not be blamed for devoting his time, his ingenuity and his name to the business of making money. In the few years which elapsed between the election of Edward Heath as Leader of the Party and the Conservative victory in 1970, Maudling managed to make no less than three unfortunate associations. Of all the opportunities available he chose for his close interest Bernie Cornfield's IOS, Jerome Hoffman's Real Estate Fund of America and lastly John Poulson and his international architects' practice.

If there was one thing these three operations had in common, other than their unhappy endings, it was their panache. Dynamism and enthusiasm made all three burn with a curiously brilliant light. Maudling was not the only one to be drawn to their flames. Of the three, Poulson and his somewhat vulgar empire would appear to be the most innocuous.

The company was the biggest architectural practice in Europe. Its fall came through bankruptcy proceedings to recover debts of a quarter of a million pounds. Maudling's name was first mentioned in connection with one of the Poulson group of companies of which he had been Chairman prior to June 1970. He had also been Chairman of two other Poulson companies. The disclosures which flooded into the press from the tightly packed court at Wakefield every Monday were, however, highly disturbing. Poulson had quite clearly been making large payments to individuals in politics and the civil service: payments which had been quite evidently connected with contracts subsequently awarded to his company.

If a shudder ran through the House of Commons at these disclosures and at the mention not only of Maudling, but of two other MPs in connection with Poulson's affairs, it must surely have been because there was little in this drama to separate it from the hundreds of dealings of Members with commercial enterprises. There, but for the grace of God... Poulson was in any case doing business in a quite normal way for the building trade. If he went about things with more energy; if he fished bigger fish with fleshier bait, he was still conforming to the general pattern. Business is inevitably done through the greasing of palms, little gifts, entertainment. These are the inducements with which those who have something to sell, influence the decisions of those who must buy.

Maudling's position as the Chairman or President of a company was above board. There are other sorts of employment which are from the start totally corrupt and they are very attractive to MPs. There was the interesting case of the MP who reported an attempt to bribe him to the Commissioner of Police. Geoffrey Rhodes said he was offered £12,000 a year bribe to persuade BEA and BOAC to switch their routes through Brindisi instead of Rome.*

The originator of the attempted bribe was believed to be the relative of an Italian Government Minister and alleged to have substantial interests in the development of the Brindisi port area. 'I met him at a cocktail party,' Rhodes told the *Sunday Times* reporter James Margach, 'shortly after he phoned me for a meeting, and when he came he suggested we go for a walk. I said I was on a three-line Whip and couldn't leave the Commons so we went to the Harcourt Room. He made the offer of a business proposition.'

The Italian told Rhodes that the British Airlines could save £200,000 a year on the 30 per cent reduction he would offer them over the Rome Airport fees. As well as this, the vast new tourist area opened up in southern Italy would interest British travel agents. It was the perfect proposition. Any doubts the MP might have had about the morality of what he was being asked to do would be assuaged by the prospect of the benefit which would accrue to British interests. Not only this but everything would be made to look proper because there was guaranteed support from

* *Sunday Times* report — August 1972.

Italian Ministerial quarters and from an Italian Bank.

The Italian may have annoyed Rhodes. In any case he reckoned without being questioned about his own interests. Bribery is a more accepted way of life in Italy and it is probable that the flexibility of Italian politicians when faced with bribes of this order was being mistakenly applied to a British situation. In answer to Rhodes technical questions about runway length and air traffic and other equipment his prospective employer said: 'Make representations to your Ministers and the chiefs of your airlines and it will be worth £1,000 a month to you — in notes or any currency you like.'

Rhodes, who has no business interests outside Parliament, was of the opinion that the Italian had heard of his interest in aviation subjects and decided to approach him. Anyone who has ever seen Brindisi airport will know that to compete with the stopover attractions of Rome, it and the tiny hick town of Brindisi would have a long way to go. No doubt, however, there are prospects for tour operators and Rhodes could have lined the vaults of his bank quite satisfactorily for very little effort.

Stranger things have happened. Indeed in local authority spheres they happen every day. If Members of Parliament accept these kinds of retainer, they do so with the utmost discretion. That the offers are available from unscrupulous sources there is no doubt. The great question is: How many of them are taken up?

A great deal depends upon the way the proposition is put to the Member. An obvious attempt to bribe does not bring about as good a reaction as the offer of a business link cemented by a directorship. It would not be fair to Mr. Rhodes to suggest that had he been offered a directorship or a business partnership worth £1,000 a month he would have accepted. But there are plenty of MPs with fewer scruples. So long as the deal looks all right on paper they feel they are in a legitimate position to canvass for business.

It is virtually impossible to carry on business activities in political life without finding that one's own interests conflict at some stage with political ones. Members of Parliament who are directors of perfectly straight companies can still find that their interests as directors will conflict at some stage with the public interest. It is then a difficult decision for the Member who must choose between continuing to earn his fees or to put his loyalties in order. Very often this depends upon the terms of his agreement.

Brian Walden, who admits to an income of over fifteen thousand a year and is experienced in these matters, says: 'The minute I feel that I am expected to carry my interests in the concern beyond the normal duties I make it quite clear that I am not prepared to comply.' He agrees: 'Yes, pressure is put upon one from time to time: one would be a fool to agree.' That some Members of Parliament do accept that they are expected to bring pressure to bear in the right quarters, is, he thinks, likely. If this is because of a straight relationship there are fewer dangers. Members of Parliament do get some very enticing offers of tax-free benefits. Lushing up goes on mainly on a small scale and occasionally on an extremely lavish level. One ex-Cabinet Minister tells of some very pleasant gifts being received by one or two leading political figures. But, as Brian Walden says, 'When they start offering flats full of girls is the moment you steer clear if you have any sense.'

Most Members do have plenty of sense as far as this is concerned, but every now and again a Member oversteps that faint line which divides apparent honesty from a suddenly brazen dishonesty. Members of Parliament tend to be sympathetic with colleagues who succumb to the temptation to over-zealously represent the interests of their paymasters. The temptation to indulge in 'silliness' or 'madness' is regarded by most MPs as ever-present for them all. The risks of overstepping the intuitive threshold between acceptable and non-acceptable behaviour seem to be higher when a political rather than a commercial cause is involved. Politics is a weakness, sometimes fatal, for all politicians. Their own views on an issue can lead them to an association with an outside pressure group or even a foreign power. If this association is reinforced by gifts or fees, then it enters that shadowy area between the honest expression of political opinion, and influence brought to bear for material gain.

The degree to which a Member of Parliament is free to espouse individual political causes must always be in question. The four MPs who were expelled from the Labour Party for their Communist sympathies in 1948–50 were clearly sincere in their beliefs. It is unlikely that they were elected for those opinions however; and since they were opinions inimical to the party on whose ticket they had reached Parliament they were clearly overstepping the mark, and their expulsion was justified.

Suspicion of fellow-travelling has been a shadow to the Labour Party in the past. These shadows walked again almost unnoticed early in 1974 with the disclosures of a highly placed defector, Joseph Frolic — a major in the Czechoslovakian intelligence service for seventeen years — to the West. Contained in a debriefing report for the CIA was the information that 'an elaborate spy-ring involving Members of Parliament, civil servants and a double-agent' had been operating in London during the sixties.

Christopher Sweeney writing in *The Times* of January 25th, 1974, gave details of an interview with Frolic in which he had said that three people, who were Members of Parliament, had received money for spying, that two of them had been recruited by Czech intelligence officers and that they had 'worked for many years and delivered important information concerning British defence potential and domestic foreign policies of the Labour Party and the British Government.'

They had not been arrested after Frolic had given their names to the CIA in July 1973 because sufficient evidence could not be found to stand up in court. 'He told me in London last week, however,' wrote Sweeney, 'that the three were confronted with the available evidence and their "usefulness was finished".' The suggestion that the three were perhaps no longer MPs was contained in the phrase: 'But the London people have other means up their sleeves to damage these men and they have already done so.'

Concern for the political and financial affiliation of MPs — and also of civil servants is not superfluous under the circumstances. Frolic went on to say that at that time in Britain: 'I knew of no other place in the world outside Austria and West

Germany where infiltration of the Government apparatus, of Parliament, of the Trade Unions and of scientific institutions was so complete and on so grand a scale as in Great Britain.' Perhaps times have changed. Or then again, perhaps not. Perhaps a further *Times* story, this time by Michael Copeland, which claimed intensification of CIA interest and activity in Britain especially with reference to Communism in Trade Unions and in political life, was yet another small smoke trace of subterfuge in the clear blue sky of British democracy.

The Public Relations Snare

It is not necessary for money to change hands for a politician to get into trouble for over-stressing certain political angles. A mixture of political sympathy and impressionability can be as good as any other attraction to the interests looking for a respectable front. Presumably this is what the Pakistan Government of Yahya Kahn was looking for when it placed the following advertisement in *The Times* of May 4th, 1971:

> Urgently wanted: a British MP to go to East Pakistan for a survey of the situation as seen by the Army and report back to the British Public. All expenses paid.

Three Members of Parliament who responded to this invitation went out during June 1971 to Pakistan. It was just one of many trips which a foreign power feels it necessary to organise when British journalists' reports are too unfavourable. One difference about this trip was the fact that one of the MPs, Mrs. Jill Knight, was to 'report back to the British public' through the medium of the *Daily Telegraph*.

Mrs. Knight was a privileged person. Yahya Khan had thrown all foreign journalists out of East Pakistan following the streams of despatches reporting brutal massacre of the Bengali Hindus by the Pakistan Army: accusations of genocide and brutality of every kind flooded into the Western press. As a result America threatened to cut off aid to Pakistan. No wonder Yahya Kahn felt he needed a public relations operation: and who better than a British MP to carry it out.

The first of Mrs. Knight's despatches appeared on the foreign page of the *Daily Telegraph* on June 16th. It set the scene for what was to follow by denying allegations that there had been discrimination against Hindus. The despatch quoted the President and made the point that the Army had been forced to act to defend the State.

The second despatch further set the scene by a 'straight' report about danger to British nationals. The report opened:

'A British planter, James Boyd, was abducted and killed by Mukti Bahini in an attack on a tea estate in East Pakistan according to authentic reports.'

The report went on to mention further attacks: 'Four British factories have been destroyed' and closed with 'Strenuous efforts are being made by "freedom fighters" from the Indian side of the border to bring work on all tea plantations in the area to a halt.' Naturally such a report would help to convince British readers of the 'wisdom' of the Pakistan Army's actions in the area.

In the third despatch on July 19th and headlined 'Evidence of Awami Atrocities', Mrs. Knight's report began:

'I have been unable to find any evidence of Army massacres during an extensive tour of East Pakistan and I am convinced that President Yahya Kahn is extremely anxious for a return to normal life there.'

She went on

'On the other hand I was appalled, after visiting a centre for 4,000 displaced persons in Dacca, by the evidence of brutality committed by extremist elements of the Awami League.'

On July 21st Mrs. Knight wrote:

'I am convinced that the people who fled from East Pakistan to India need not now be afraid to return to their homes.

President Yahya Kahn and the Pakistan Army are doing

everything possible to ensure a return to normal life.

This became apparent during a two-hour discussion in Rawalpindi with President Yahya before I flew back to London.'

On July 23rd the *Telegraph* carried the first report by its reporter, Claire Hollingsworth. Miss Hollingsworth was among the first small group to be allowed back into the Eastern Province when President Yahya lifted his ban. Miss Hollingsworth's report appeared on the front page. On the foreign page was a surprise despatch from Mrs. Knight, now back in Birmingham. Owing to 'an error in the transmission' of her July 21st despatch Mrs. Knight wanted to make it clear that she had not said it was safe for refugees to return to their homes. What she had said, ran the July 23rd story, was:

'President Yahya Khan and his military and civil heads of staff are doing everything possible to make the return safe.'

'I am not,' wrote Mrs. Knight, 'in fact yet certain that all returning refugees would be quite safe.'

Those who remember the bloody massacres that followed in the period after these despatches will be surprised at Mrs. Knight's judgment. Even the *Daily Telegraph* leader of the same July 23rd issue felt obliged to say at the time:

'President Yahya Kahn's statement that life had sufficiently returned to normal for the refugees to return home is not borne out by the first reports of our special correspondent Claire Hollingsworth. In the countryside she reports fear and hatred of the Western Government and passive resistance.'

In the same issue of the same paper Mrs. Knight's article included the following remarks:

'I now believe that a clever and highly effective propaganda campaign is being waged against Pakistan.'

The most interesting statement of all followed:

'Many people have been duped with false information.'

Perhaps one of them was Mrs. Knight.

Public relations is one of the great snares of politics. There are a number of organisations presenting themselves to prospective clients as specialists in political public relations. This is an activity that most foreign powers indulge in whenever necessary; sometimes with and sometimes without professional public relations specialists.

One of the essentials for any political public relations man is a fat wallet: with this he offers retainers to one or two MPs, preferably one from each side. The PR man may be working for a trade union, not represented in the House, for a pressure group, for a charity, for a foreign power, or even a company that likes to have grass roots political influence. There is not much wrong in this on the surface. It is another one of those nebulous and shadowy areas with the unsavoury flavour that adheres to all paid lobbying.

During the late sixties there was a fuss about an MP who, it was alleged, had been paid by a public relations consultant to lobby for the then new and nasty Greek Junta. The Greek Junta was very unpopular in Britain. Greek democracy was a special case; and although no one had done very much to try and improve the state of the democracy while it actually still existed, there was an outcry when the Colonels took over. It was a much bigger outcry than any that has accompanied the arrival of colonels to any other seat of power. Refugees of high social standing all seemed to make their way to Britain and the British press was filled with reports of the wicked colonels. Public relations was therefore much in demand as far as Britain was concerned and the Junta found themselves a promising consultant to do the job.

Scandal came in the autumn of 1968 shortly after five British MPs and their wives had enjoyed a visit to Greece at the invitation of the new régime. The *Sunday Times* Insight team had unearthed several documents originating from the offices of the Public Relations consultant for the Junta, Maurice Fraser. Fraser had a contract for £100,000 a year, and to justify it he had written up some interesting proposals containing suggestions such as that of setting up an Anglo-Greek Association in London, which would 'be sponsored by government supporters in London, but not apparently so. Its purpose would be mainly political . . .'

When the *Sunday Times* team obtained a copy of Fraser's fifth report to the Junta, they interviewed him. He replied by taking out an injunction to stop the paper from publishing the report. On October 6th, 1968, the *Sunday Times* published a full report of the PR man Fraser's activities in connection with the Junta, following the discontinuation of the injunction by the Appeal Court. One of the fantastic and disturbing claims made by Fraser in his fifth report was that among his staff was 'A British MP — he works behind the scenes in order to influence other MPs.'

The *Sunday Times* dismissed this claim, with many of Fraser's others, as being bravado, 'and simply untrue'. Nevertheless they interviewed the five MPs, who had succumbed to Fraser's persuasion thus allowing him to enjoy the triumph of getting them to Greece. The MPs were doing no more than any other MPs who go on trips to dubious régimes, mainly for the ride. But the dangers of doing so were considerable. As one of the MPs, Gordon Bazier, told the *Sunday Times*: 'The Members on this trip were put in a difficult position. Certainly I am. There have been one or two versions of what has or what has not been said.'

The other four all denied that Fraser had tried to put any pressure on them or had, in the words of Russell Johnson, 'tried to pull the wool over my eyes'. Only one MP had previously had any connection with the PR firm. David Webster, then MP for Weston-super-Mare, had known Howard Preece, Fraser's senior staff man, since he was, said Webster, 'Chairman — or a leading Member of my YC's.'

The trip may have been harmless enough. The MPs may not have been prevailed upon to make any particularly approving noises about the régime. As Anthony Buck, one of the five, said to the Insight reporter: 'If there had been any improper approach to me, I certainly would have cracked down on it and taken action.' He added, 'There was no impropriety on behalf of Fraser.' Nevertheless the fact remains, Fraser was himself capable of using the MP's visit to make the régime respectable. That, after all, was its purpose. The Greek Junta was not a charity trying to improve the minds of British MPs in the interests of dispassionate truth.

The régime were clearly not displeased with the visit of the five MPs. (As Insight reported — 'They afterwards spoke very favourably about the régime'.) The same five were invited to return in October for the National Referendum the Junta was holding, to show the world that it was in power by democratic vote. Anyone who had been to Greece and wandered around freely would know that this could only be a joke. Yet five more MPs were invited to accompany the original five. All spoke to their Whip's offices and gained approval for the trip. Ostensibly they were there as observers. Yet no one returned to publicly condemn the Referendum and there was no doubt in my mind, that the Junta was unwelcome to say the least to a considerable number of Greeks. The Referendum, however, indicated over 90 per cent support. The Greeks are still laughing: but what of the British MPs.

Whether Fraser had an MP on his staff or not, the activities which he had pledged himself to indulge in clearly pointed in the same direction. His claim that: 'We have to protect the identity of the British MP otherwise he would be exposed', may have been nothing more than bluff. But he was running very close to the wind by adding: 'But his name is at the disposal of the [Greek] Prime Minister.'

The *Sunday Times* suggested that 'a more formidable operator working on the same lines might be harder to expose and neutralise. Before one comes along, Parliament might consider the evidence of the Fraser case as an additional argument for the proposition that political lobbyists should be openly registered by law in Britain as they are in the United States.'

There is now a Select Committee on Members' Interests. The inference is that Members should perhaps be asked to declare their interests, so that rumours such as the Fraser one cannot be put about. If political lobbyists were registered, the Committee would at least know where to look for evidence that such a declaration is necessary. But declaration or registration do not preclude the possibility that dishonest operators would not continue to practise. Again, even when a Member's interests are no secret, he can run into trouble.

One casualty of her own public relations activities on behalf of the Palestinian Arabs was Mrs. Margaret McKay. Mrs. McKay, a public relations consultant, had represented Clapham for Labour since 1964. On May 6th, 1970, the morning papers carried reports of her resignation. The front page of *The Times* carried a version of the resignation story in which Mrs. McKay declared she had been denied the right to defend herself against accusations. Reg Underhill, of the Transport House Candidates' department, said that Mrs. McKay resigned before the meeting could be held which would have given her the opportunity to reply to her accusers.

The original unrest in the Clapham Labour Party began over Mrs. McKay's connections with the Arab League. 'Later,' says Underhill, 'other criticisms of Mrs. McKay's conduct as a Member of Parliament were added.' The row with the constituency party came after months, in which rumour after rumour about Mrs. McKay's Arab associations drifted about in London's rather incestuous political circles. Mrs. McKay herself had made no effort to conceal any aspect of her association: she frequently visited the Arab countries, and was showered with expensive gifts. That Mrs. McKay sincerely believed in the Arab cause was in no doubt. In *The Times* report she was quoted as follows:

'My fight has been in support of the Arab's right to resist the invasion and spoilation of their homelands: also in defence of the ancient rights of MPs fearlessly to speak the truth.'

The dangers of being too closely associated with any one cause are clearly illustrated by Mrs. McKay's experience. Whether the association is purely mercenary or, as in the case of Mrs. McKay, stemming from a sincere political belief, the pitfall is to bang the drum too loud. The result, justifiable or not, is a natural suspicion: and in consequence what Mrs. McKay called, 'a campaign of public abuse and humiliation against me', is thought of in terms of, 'no smoke without a fire'.

Secret Payrolls

When any incident occurs which throws doubt on the integrity of a Member of Parliament, all Members fall under its shadow. Consequently, corruption is suspected where none is to be found. I recently spoke to a responsible businessman who was convinced that the behaviour of a leading Labour politician on the Common Market was a result of 'nobbling'. There were city rumours, I was told to the effect that this man had 'been got at' by companies whose interests would be much enhanced by British entry to the EEC.

To politicians who still have the hope of power, this sort of nobbling would be frank foolishness. To those who have no prospect of power or who find wealth preferable to what power they already hold, a bribe is more attractive. And — the higher one's position, the greater is the influence and the higher the price. At the other end of the scale there is also the fact that back-benchers who have no additional source of income may be anxious to acquire one: perhaps over-anxious.

The case of Wil Owen stems from exactly this sort of situation. Owen was accused of a total of eight charges, five of which were for passing information to a foreign power and three for committing acts preparatory to communicating information. Again the main evidence and the principle snare was that money had changed hands. Owen's story was that he first received money from a Czechoslovakian Embassy official in return for an article to be published in an East European magazine. Owen was first asked to do this at an Embassy cocktail party. He received £25 for his trouble. In the hope that he would be asked to write further articles, he maintained the contact with the Embassy man: and this is where the well-oiled trap began to close about him. He accepted further money; he met his contact for lunch and dinner: the classic espionage net was being woven.

At the trial Owen said: 'I was used for ulterior purposes and I regret being such a fool.' The start had been innocent enough. Then as the small amounts of money, 'Sometimes it was ten pounds, sometimes twenty-five', were paid over to him, he was asked questions about various aspects of the British military position including BAOR and the chieftain tank.

Owen had tried to get out of the arrangement whereby the Czechoslovak representative came to the House and ostensibly talked to him about trade matters: but he had been threatened with exposure to MI5. Rather than make a confession he had allowed the noose to tighten further and gone on accepting the meagre payments that he was offered.

Owen was acquitted. He was an elderly man and the affair in any case marked the end of an undistinguished career on the back-benches. Any danger of important secrets being given away was limited as Owen himself illustrated during cross-examination. He said: 'You tell me where any ordinary back-bench MP, except as a Member of the Estimates Committee, can learn anything of a confidential nature.' However true this is of the majority, there is always the danger — and for the paymaster, always the hope — that sometime somewhere the informed gossip of Westminster will produce a valuable piece of knowledge.

Owen was a man who admitted to having taken an interest in Eastern Europe. His interest was no doubt evidenced by his presence at a Czech Embassy cocktail party. His case was a pathetic and unfortunate example of the ease with which an MP can succumb, however innocently, to the temptations around him. An MP with more than a casual interest in Eastern Europe could get on to an Embassy payroll even more easily than Owen. Like Mrs. McKay, his political enthusiasms could lead him into active support.

Support for Arabs, Jews, white Rhodesian or black South Africans taken too far could lead to the same constituency problems as those experienced by Mrs. McKay: support for a Warsaw Pact country could be a security risk and is therefore in quite a different category. The interest in any Eastern European country has to be expressed with care, not only because of our own nervous security network. The dangers of any association with a power of this sort are illustrated by Owen. Blackmail will be used, if necessary, to ensure that the friendly interest remains a valuable working relationship.

Most MPs are very careful not to get themselves into situations of the kind that ended the career of Wil Owen. 'He must have been mad,' was the comment one MP made to me.

The different between Wil Owen and an MP who accepts payment from a commercial concern for advice, is really only one of emphasis. Yet that emphasis is all-important. A Member, who accepts a retainer from a commercial concern to advise them when called upon to do so, is in a sense, 'committing an act preparatory to communicating information' in the same way as Owen was. There is no proof that information would be any more valuable to the Warsaw Pact countries, than knowledge of some Government plans would be to a company like Rio Tinto Zinc. In the lives of ordinary people a big ruthless company can be just as big a danger in the long run as the East Germans or the Poles. It is the existence of a cold war which makes the difference: and anyone who flirts with 'the other side' is living very dangerously indeed.

The more influential a politician is, the more dangerously he has to live. Absolute honesty is hard to find in the world. Amongst the perplexing galaxy of pressures operating in Parliament any vested interest can take its chance of support somewhere. Most Members will keep away from anything that jeopardises their position in public life. Occasionally, however, someone goes off the rails. It has happened in all the instances mentioned above to a varying degree. It has happened on other occasions and it will continue to happen. For all the Members that, to use Charles Pannell's words, 'get found out in this place', there may however be many more who do not. The risk of pushing for an interest which is undeclared is only in being found out.

The thin and wavy line that MPs tread can sometimes be hard to see for Members and for the public. It is possible that the bulk of Members are more honest than anyone imagines. While interests do not have to be declared, the doubt is always there. To an honest MP an enforced declaration of interests could seem like an insult to his integrity. To the public it is merely a safeguard. It would be better to know, for instance, that when a powerful Labour Minister supported a Uranium deal with South Africa he was free of all interest in the company which benefited. It would be valuable to know the relationship of the same Minister with the same company when he is also seen to be supporting that company's application to carry out open-cast mining in a British National Park. It is not that all MPs are dishonest. It is not even that a few of them are completely dishonest. It is simply that some of them are less than honest for some of the time. The public have a right to know who swings the pendulum and why.

It will never be possible to examine all the complex reasons why Members push for a particular interest. It is, however, in the public interest that the massive power of the business world should be seen for what it is. A Member does not have to be in the pay of a specific company to operate in their interest. He may, like one Conservative MP I know, be an ardent worker for settlement with the White Rhodesian minority because of his substantial family investments in Rhodesian business. He may, like Norman St. John Stevas, be opposed to the Abortion Reform Act because he is a Roman Catholic: he may, like Douglas Jay, be opposed to British Membership of the EEC because he hates 'le continent' and foreign flavours.

Whereas commercial interests can be declared, little whimsies, like loathing Rome or loving Monte Carlo, which may be powerful forms of influence, cannot. The latter instances cannot, however, be called corrupt: and although most MPs are never more than mildly corrupt it is best to know why, if bent at all, they bend a certain way.

Part IV

THE PRIVATE MEMBER

I

A VERY UNPLEASANT LIFE

Ben Whittaker, ex-MP, says of politics: 'It's a very unpleasant life.' Many would agree with him: Parliamentary life may have its advantages. There may be powers and pleasure, exhilaration and reward: but for the man who has his own interests, who has private pursuits, sports and relationships to follow Parliament is a grossly disruptive life.

Not all Members of Parliament look for interest outside politics. Perhaps one of the main features of politicians is that they cannot leave politics alone. It is life-blood, bread and pleasure to them. Like self-made millionaires, they get no interest from anything except getting on with the job. John Gorst says, 'I get bored easily.' In that he is fairly typical. Politics is full of people with itchy personalities; those who cannot find their personal peace without activity. Harold Wilson was a good example during his first premiership of a man who cannot leave his work alone. He might have been a better Prime Minister had he spent more time on a golf course and less in booby-trapping his Cabinet. The ability to relax is important in high-pressure jobs.

But there are people in politics who are well rounded, who like the pleasanter things in life. Many of them may confine their interests to the flesh-pots: but there are also those who look for diversion in the form of a home life and the relationships that more ordinary mortals take for granted. But politics does not afford much opportunity for spare-time pursuits.

The Parliamentary term runs theoretically for thirty-four weeks a year, with nearly twenty weeks of the year unaccounted for, MPs would seem to be well off for holidays.

But, as Norman Atkinson says, 'Anyone who thinks Members of Parliament only work thirty-four weeks in a year has only to go along to Westminister in September to find out how wrong that is.'

Irregularity probably takes more toll of MP's leisure than the actual hours — though these are long enough for the dedicated. A few late-night sittings, especially those with dawn rising, can play havoc with health and strength — to say nothing of married life: for where, after all, are a Member's wife and children while he lies abed in the morning catching up on his beauty sleep.

Then there are other stresses. A major one is travel. Members' visit their constituency at week-ends — and half of them have seats in constituencies over four hours' journey away from Westminster. One-third of MPs have their homes neither in London nor in their constituencies. So for them the travel involved is around three sides of a triangle.

In orbit most of the week-ends and some of the week — for there are other trips and journeys to make — the Member may also have to drive himself over several hundreds of miles. Members with large rural constituencies have longer but possibly more scenic driving than those with urban areas to nurse, but even so driving is a considerable stress factor in the lives of MPs. About half of the Members drive around ten thousand miles a year and about one-sixth drive over twenty thousand miles. Some are luckier than others and have constituency minions to chauffeur them around. On the whole this is rare and even wives have other duties. The Member has to do his own driving: and as medical research has shown, the physical reactions gone through in car driving (raised blood-pressure, adrenalin in the blood) are comparable with high stress situations.

Members of Parliament suffer from stress more than from any other illness. A survey carried out in the last Parliament was instituted after the sudden rash of deaths from heart disease among MPs during the 1964–66 period.* As a result of

* Wright and Pincherle: *Life and Work in the House of Commons*, British Heart Foundation Report.

the survey the authors discovered some interesting facts. Among them that suicide accounts for a higher than average number of deaths in the MP population than in the population as a whole.* Although suicide is an indication, among other things, of stress in operation, there were other symptoms which were more precise indications of stress. For instance headaches, rheumatism, fatigue, irritability, indigestion and muscular pain. MPs suffer from all of these with reasonable regularity.

Politics is a tense sort of life. Much sitting and waiting and a fair amount of suppressed passion for those who really feel their politics. Norman Atkinson says that, 'for the committed political animal', the stresses created by Parliamentary frustration are almost unbearable at times.

Perhaps the high stress factor accounts for the reputation Members have acquired for being on the whole heavy drinkers. In this case it may come as a surprise to learn that in the same survey 7 per cent of MPs recorded themselves as non-drinkers. On the other hand, there are a number of what can only be described as drunken bums amongst Members of Parliament. A fair number of MPs do drink heavily and as one Member told me: 'Drink is one of the hazards of this place.'

Bars are, after all, a part of any system of socialising and a good place to go if one wants to chat to people. Getting the lie of the land is part of the Member's activity and he is more likely to learn items of interest over a drink or two than he is over the sobering aroma of a cup of House of Commons coffee.

Hanging around is one of the curses of the politician's job as it is of the journalists. Drink is a part of that. A Member may not be doing very much in the House but he is often obliged to remain. Divisions come fast and furious at times when Bills are going through clause by clause. In any case Whips decree that the MPs should at least be at hand, if not actually in the debate. A very small number of Members have any sort of home within division bell distance from the House. Six minutes are all that are allowed to get from wherever into the

* Wright and Pincherle: *Mortality of Members of Parliament.*

lobby. Three of those could be spent negotiating corridors of the House.

The demands of the Whips are a great inconvenience to Members. Whilst waiting around for a division even if not requested 'to be in attendance for the whole of the debate', the Member can hardly go home and put his feet up, kiss his children good night, or go to bed with his mistress. Perhaps Members of Parliament, like the ladies of the guillotine, should take up knitting.

Planning their lives with the aid of the Whip, Members can fit in a little sport and recreating if they try very hard. Ted Heath is the most celebrated swimmer at present in the House, and this is one sport at least which is possible for Westminster-bound fitness fiends. But there are not many MPs who keep fit. Surprisingly few of them ever fall ill. Nevertheless the amount of exercise taken by Members is comparatively little. Some MPs take less than half an hour's walking a day — the minimum required to maintain reasonable health. If pre-occupied with their weight, as many MPs are, they do very little about it, even at week-ends.

But politics is sport to most Members of Parliament. Other interests — art, culture, literature are fitted in where there is time. Members do at least have one night a week off from the Whips when they are paired and can take their wives or girl-friends to the theatre. For the London Member there is a little more opportunity to indulge a taste for metropolitan life. The others are only too glad to get away from the city, even if for many of them it is to far less congenial parts of the country.

Personal Relationships

Oliver Cromwell wrote to his wife from Ireland: '... Thou art dearer to me than any living creature.' Yet they were separated most of the time after Cromwell took up politics. Such is the lot of many modern political marriage partners.

Sometimes the separation is very hard to bear: Conservative MPs in the Macmillan era used to sing a little ditty called 'waiting for Hugh', of which one variant began as follows:

> Waiting for Hugh,
> Waiting for Hugh,
> I've nothing to do,
> So I'm waiting for Hugh.

It seems that the young wife of one of the Members used to sit tearfully waiting for her darling husband in the Central Lobby. Her inevitable reply to whomsoever greeted her was what formed the basis of the song.

Not all wives are so attached to their husbands that they follow them around waiting in the hope of seeing them. There are, no doubt, many grass widows of managing directors and other busy men who would like to hang about in their husband's offices waiting to catch a glimpse of them; but they would no doubt be made quickly aware that they were compromising a brilliant career. A wife is a wife and must by definition remain in the background. Depending on the level of the relationship and perhaps also its duration, wives will be more or less happy at the absences of their husbands from the domestic scene.

Parliament rather more than other ways of life, except perhaps for journalism, puts strains on domestic harmony: and especially where this was based on a conventional routine. Parliament is not a regular life. In some ways it does have a regular pattern: but this fits in so badly with the more usual nine-to-five routine of other people that it could have an intensely disruptive effect upon any marriage. This, of course, depends very much on the way the non-Parliamentary marriage partner reacts to the set-up. The reaction, in turn, probably has a lot to do with the stage at which the Parliamentary routine first impinges on the marriage.

Broadly speaking, there seem to be four types of wife associated with Parliament. Apart from the wife who is herself an MP either with her husband in Parliament or not, there are three main types: the quiet retiring wife who plays no part in her husband's political activities; the active political wife who takes a major interest in her husband's Parliamentary career:

and the otherwise active wife who pursues separate interests of her own. Of these, it is probably the quiet woman who most wants her husband to herself and who is most likely to resent the demands his Parliamentary career makes on their domestic relationship. This type of wife may also feel that certain duties are thrust upon her. She may even, in certain cases, be obliged to go through the motions of keeping the marriage respectable for the sake of her husband's career when she would really prefer a divorce.

Duty is the dominating factor in Parliamentary wifeliness, whichever way we look at the subject. The wife who takes an active interest in her husband's political career may be just as deprived of her husband's company as the mousy lady, but her duty and very probably her love affects her less selfishly. She wants wholeheartedly to help and support her husband in every possible way. Probably no truer examples of the classic wife as 'strong woman behind successful man' can be found than among the spouses of Members of Parliament.

However dutiful or however strong any of these women are, there is no reason to imagine their life to be entirely noble sacrifice. Joy Pardoe, wife of John Pardoe, told me that she knew of several examples of wives who, in the words of her husband, 'queen it over their husband's constituencies'. Status is something an MPs wife has that does appeal to ambitious women. Some of the tough ladies of politics are wives and not MPs: they work through their husbands, who undoubtedly consult them on many political problems.

The lady who was waiting for Hugh is a good example of the woman who does not actively help her husband's career. How many Members of Parliament have wives of this sort is impossible to tell. Age groups seem to be no means of separating the wife types from each other: but it is probably reasonable to say that the Member who enters the House at the age of 40 or over is more likely to have a troubled domestic life than one who starts his career in his late twenties or early thirties. At this early stage his marriage is more capable of adapting, and a wife who, like Mrs. Ben Whittaker, married a Parliamentary candidate knows exactly what she is in for from the beginning. It can hardly be easy for a wife who for twelve or fifteen years has waved her husband off at nine or so, and received him back in the early evening to get used to seeing him once a week at week-ends and then only at meal-times if she is lucky.

This is where independent wives with their own interests can probably be the most acceptable for a busy and erratic man. Demands on a Member for his personal company are probably less cloying where the wife is wholly able to amuse herself with cultural or business pursuits. Reunions between such people are more likely to take the form of a delicious escape from the cares of public life than the meetings between the more dependent wives and their husbands.

One Member who has been in the House for fifteen years told me that the relationship with his wife had benefited from their periods of separation. As almost anyone knows, a dull routine often dulls people's responses to each other. A more looked forward to once a week meeting has more of a sparkle, than the daily return from some commuter train to a repetitive welcome of the 'Had a good day at the office, dear,' type. No doubt the parallel 'Had a good week at Parliament, dear,' also exists: but it has the advantage of being listened to once rather than five times a week.

Two MPs who have their homes in constituencies over 400 miles from London, one in his thirties and one in his fifties both claim to be happily married and certainly have every appearance of being in love with their wives. Both are married to very independent and characterful ladies, one of whom has her own cultural interests and the other being a devoted political wife.

For the family-minded MP the problem of maintaining his marriage and bringing up his children with some degree of normality is severe. Of the 630 Members of Parliament, two-thirds actually have their family homes outside London and half well beyond commuting distance. Week-ends are the only times they can get to see their wives and their children. This sometimes means that they are strangers to them.

John Pardoe is one MP who, in spite of the fact that his constituency is North Cornwall, decided after much wrangling to have his family home in London, and this entirely so that his children could grow up 'in as normal a family environment as possible'.

The whole question of the effect of Parliamentary life on the children of Members of Parliament is an open one. It requires a sociological study to provide any foundation of fact to what is, after all, only an assumption — that the absence of the father from the family home has a bad effect on the development of the child.

The Pardoes are quite definite about the bad effects of leading a separated life. Rupert Pardoe was three years old when his father began commuting from North Cornwall constituency to London every Monday. The snag in the whole arrangement, says Pardoe, was the fact that even though he could spend his week-end in the same district as his family he had very little time in their company. 'It was,' he says, 'thoroughly unsatisfactory and hopeless for family life.' Mrs. Pardoe says, 'John had to dash off to do things, and Saturday was a washout.' Pardoe himself says that 'Although we tried to keep Sunday as a family day, people used to call simply because they knew they would find me at home.'

The worse aspect was the effect Pardoe's two-centre life had on his eldest son Rupert. When I asked Rupert what he thought of his father not being at home much when they lived in Cornwall he answered: 'It didn't really matter.' 'But,' says John Pardoe, 'Rupert does not remember that he used to cry every Sunday night when I went to get the sleeper back to London.'

The Pardoes took a brave decision and moved the family to London, the children live a 'normal' life where Daddy is at least home for breakfast every day. The strains imposed on John Pardoe are only slightly alleviated. He still does two night-sleeper rides a week. But at least 'I am home after breakfast on Sunday,' he says.

The Pardoes now have three children, all of whom go to school in Hampstead. Another contrast with North Cornwall is revealed, in the comment of Rupert that: 'No one takes much notice of the fact that I have an MP for my Daddy.' As Pardoe says, 'In Hampstead everyone's Daddy is something.' But Mrs. Pardoe recalls that this is not so in Cornwall. 'Some of the children,' she says, 'were very unpleasant to Rupert during the Election.' Some Conservative children made war. And Rupert himself admits, 'Some of the boys were definitely rather envious of me because my father was a Member of Parliament.'

Now that the Pardoes live a family life, there are not too many disadvantages to be overcome. As far as the children are concerned life is relatively normal. They will not admit to any special feelings for the House of Commons, though little Tania Pardoe says she enjoys having dinner in the House. The boys, however, remain resolutely, and rather over-emphatically unimpressed.

David Steel is another devoted family MP whose family and children live in his constituency. Steel hates London and this is why he elected to leave his family at home in Scotland. Now, however, he is beginning to have regrets. His children are getting to the age where he notices and they notice his absence from them. It is indeed tragic that an MP should have to choose between his personal happiness and his political career, as did Christopher Chataway. Chataway said in the late spring of 1974 that he would not stand for Parliament again and wrote a revealing article in The Sunday Times (April 21st) about the demands of politics on his time and its obliteration of his private life.

The dangers are for any MP that even the brief times he has for his children are not enough. Joy Pardoe says: 'The sort of time most wives have their husbands around is when I miss John most. For instance, to take the boys to a football match on a Saturday.' In spite of their dissatisfactions neither the Steels nor the Pardoes would part with politics. Theirs is a relatively happy story, however. Not so many MPs are lucky enough to have such happy domestic arrangements as these two. Often Members who like their private lives are really only reluctantly in politics. Ben Whittaker, for instance, clearly prefers family life to Parliament. His dilemma is that, like all political animals, he cannot stay out of politics. The political life and a love of private bliss are not compatible.

Ben Whittaker says that the most delightful aspect of losing his seat in the 1970 Election was the opportunity the event gave him of 'rediscovering my children. Both my children,' he says, 'were born during my first two years at the House — the awful phase of night-shift sittings brought about by the flood of panic legislation between 1964 and 1966. During this time,' he says, 'I could not even see them in the mornings because I was asleep.' A hard life, politics for the family man.

Norman Atkinson does not believe in politicians having children. 'None of the Left in Parliament have children,' he says. 'Hostages to fortune,' according to the tenet of Francis Bacon, are the way he sees a family in political life. 'It is not fair,' he says, 'to involve children in all this.' The wives of left-wing MPs are, according to Atkinson, as dedicated to the political cause as the Members themselves. 'Children have no place in such a life.'

Mrs. Barbara Castle once said that a woman has to choose between a successful career in politics and having children. But Mrs. Shirley Williams could prove her wrong. Mrs. Williams, a rising star on the Labour Front Bench, had a three year old daughter when she entered the House. Throughout the sixties, when the child was growing up, Mrs. Williams would go home briefly to her Kensington flat to see her daughter to bed.

But the scarcity of mothers in Parliament is a comment on the lack of ease with which maternity and politics coexist. In the 1970–74 Parliament Shirley Williams and Bernadette Macalisky were the sole representatives of motherhood: and late in the proceedings they were joined by Mrs. Margo MacDonald, a mother of two small girls following a 1973 by-election in Glasgow Govan.

Mrs. MacDonald, had she survived the February 1974 Election, would have been a fascinating guinea-pig for all those students of the sociological consequences of being a political parent. Mrs. MacDonald was lucky: her publican husband, she said, 'had known what he was doing' when he married her. She had 'always been political' and if there was a bonus now to her activities it was that they at least reaped a Parliamentary salary. Candidature itself is a severe problem to a mother. The only additional snag to actually getting elected is that one would naturally keep rather strange hours: and women MPs and candidates are now in the vanguard of those insisting that the anti-social hours by which the House itself operates must be changed.

But if working from 2.30 until 10 p.m. or later is as bad for women MPs as the same shift for working-class mothers, and thus equally as bad for their children, the male Members of Parliament, although in the majority, are not unanimously in favour of a change. One of the reasons, according to Mrs. Renée Short, is that the women can be used as committee fodder in the mornings when the men are off at their extra-curricular affairs. Women tend to be less attractive to the profferers of directorships and consultancies and therefore are over-represented on the committees because fewer men are available.

If the hours of the House are ever brought into line with twentieth century time-tables there may even be some male MPs in favour: the family men, in particular, would welcome the opportunity to lead a normal domestic life and even the single would benefit from being free to socialise at the same time as everyone else. But, even so, the Members who keep their family homes way out of town would need to rethink their life style. Margo MacDonald is one very good example of a Member who would find it difficult to move her home to London. If the fact of her being a Scottish Nationalist did not contradict London residency, the additional fact that her husband's livelihood was in Scotland sealed her difficulties. Perhaps the solution posed by her younger $7\frac{1}{2}$ year old daughter would have suited Margo MacDonald best: Mrs. MacDonald's going to London for three days a week was, said this child, 'A bit of an inconvenience for her,' and 'Why can't we have one [a Parliament] here?'

If Margo MacDonald was lucky, again it was because her husband was happy enough to welcome the children home from school and generally share domestic chores. But the equality between the sexes which would make possible the freedom of women from the assumption that marriage is bondage is still a long way off. One sign that times may be changing was when one of my fellow contestants for a constituency in 1974 gave his profession as house husband adding 'My wife earns more than I could, so I stay home and look after the children.' To my amusement he was asked one of the classic woman-pinning questions: 'Who will look after the children if you get selected or even elected?'

Role-sharing is becoming more widespread and most men still require the conventional trappings of malehood — i.e. a subservient female in tow — before they can feel sufficiently sure of themselves as men. But male or female, the right spouse can be a great help to a busy politician. Although only about half the female content of Parliament are married, many of them have husbands who, like Bernard Short (Renée Short's husband) or Ted Castle married to Barbara Castle, are politicians' *manqué* themselves. Probably male MPs also benefit from politically interested partners.

Some would have had political careers of their own had they not married first. Mrs. Ben Whittaker says modestly that she would have been more likely to go into politics herself if 'I was any good at public speaking'. She met her husband at Oxford at a party where, she says, 'We got into an argument and he rather irritated me.' It was a political argument. Ben Whittaker says that when he got married his wife 'knew exactly what she was in for'. Mrs. Whittaker is not the sort of woman who would put a career of her own before her husband and children. As a result she remains very much in the background except for 'committees and things', until election time. The Labour Party makes less social use of the Member's wife than the Conservative and Liberal Parties. In the Liberal Party the shortage of Parliamentary names gives wives a celebrity value equivalent to their MP husbands. Mrs. Laura Grimmond and Mrs. Lubbock were always as much in demand as their husbands for speech-making at constituency lunches and meetings.

The Conservative Party wives are used less as political commodity. But some intensely political women have married Conservative MPs. Mrs. Andrew Bowden was an ardent Conservative Party worker and very active politically before she met her husband. She has remained equally active after her marriage to Bowden, who thinks he won the seat, a tough marginal, through her help. The Bowdens were affianced shortly before the General Election of 1970, and Mrs. Bowden was an indispensable aide to her husband during the course of the campaign. Bowden says that he and his fiancée used to canvas streets together, she on one side, he on the other. It seems that the introductory line of 'Good afternoon, I am the fiancée of your Conservative candidate Andrew Bowden,' is as good an opener as 'Good afternoon, I am Andrew Bowden.' Mrs. Bowden is now a devoted better half to her husband in his role as dedicated constituency man. Bowden inherited his constituency of Brighton Kemptown from Dennis Hobden, one of the MPs best known to his constituents of any in the country. Unfortunately Hobden's divorce was also well known to his constituents and it may have been enough to add to the already substantial swing to the Tories and lose the seat to the man who was no less a good constituency man than he. Bowden believes absolutely in the work he does for individual constituents and his wife is the resident part of the team. While he is up at Westminster playing away, Mrs. Bowden is out and about in Kemptown meeting constituents, being tackled by them on the streets and making a note of all the local grievances she gets to hear about in the shops and markets.

A second version of themselves, able to represent them in certain circumstances and holding the fort in their absence, is what most MPs want. A wife is so often the perfect servant: and so much more so because she is able, through her love and devotion, and the fact that she may well be a talented and able individual in her own right, to truly serve her husband. Her interests are his interests and she is far better at carrying through her loyalty than any paid agent, organiser or secretary — so long as the price — that of returned love — continues to be paid.

Perhaps Mrs. Bowden is a little more than most Conservative local associations require from a Member's wife. The Conservative Party's habit of including wives in their interviews for candidates is well known; and it has been frequently commented upon. When Richard Luce was selected as Conservative candidate for the Arundel and Shoreham by-election, no secret was made of the fact that the wives were, in this instance, crucial to the final selection. It is possible that when two candidates look equally suitable the nature of their wives may become critical. Mrs. Richard Luce was selected and her husband is now MP for Shoreham (new seat since February 1974). Bill Elliott, at Central Office, says that the constituency had wanted a change after having a bachelor Member for years. When Captain Kirby died they made it clear that what they wanted was 'a nice young wife'; 'someone for the fêtes and things'. This, it appears, is the lady's role. But it is no use pretending that all wives of Conservative Members take kindly to their role as ancillary to their husband's career. Some, says William Elliott, 'absolutely hate it'. Some wives, it is true, are never heard of, but others, even the wives of Labour Members like Mrs. Caroline Wedgwood Benn, frequently do public things like opening exhibitions or attending first nights and charity performances. Wives in this role should be snappy dressers: but not too snappy. Jeans, beads and kaftan are hardly the sort of thing the wives of Members are expected to wear. It is possible that there are occasional painful scenes in Members' households over what the lady member of the team proposes to wear to open the garden party or to grace the local knees-up.

One of the expected qualities of a political wife should be dress sense. The sort of man who chooses his wife as an aid to his own success will make certain that she has dress sense among her attributes. But men who go to Parliament after some years of marriage may not have made the best selection. The ideal wife to help a political career along may be a rather different package from the ordinary run of wives.

Political, as opposed to socially graceful, wives are potentially dangerous. The day may come when they start making their own political remarks rather than mouthing only those preferred by their beloved husbands. If political and marital control should break down simultaneously the results could be disastrous. The mind boggles at the thought of a scene between husband and wife where the woman of the duo announces her intention to stand for Parliament for one of the other parties. No such delightful news story has happened yet, perhaps because love between two political creatures has to include total agreement on their mutual ethos. Time and Women's Lib will tell. There have been husband-and-wife teams in Parliament: but the Dunwoodys and the Kerrs both had similar political colours to their partners.

There are the wives one never hears of but are there when crisis looms, like brave Mrs. Valerie Profumo, and like the long-suffering wives of our Prime Ministers. Lady Churchill comes particularly to mind, but Mrs. Harold Wilson cannot be far behind her in the stakes for public admiration. Far, far more is required in patience and stamina of these women than choosing new curtains for Number Ten. Wifely qualities which can never be measured by outsiders include love, devotion, patience and consideration: the ability to comfort and support a tired and temporarily despondent husband: the capacity to help him take a difficult decision: in short all the feminine attributes. Probably the best sort of wife that an MP should have is a charming, energetic, patient, loving and only mildly political woman: one who understands politics but never interferes. If she types, is good with people, is pretty, has social graces (and perhaps even a degree in sociology if he is Labour) she should do an admirable job.

However useful a wife may be to an MP life is not much fun for her. Apart from the few intensely home-loving MPs — often the younger Members married to women of their own intellectual level, who clearly enjoy married life and make every effort to be with their wives and children, MPs are not the most likely candidates for happy marriage.

Over two-thirds of MPs live away from their wives all week. Expected to stay at home, isolated from their husbands and his work, wives can hardly be delighted at their situation. Naturally younger wives will resent the disruption to their sex and social life.

For Members who have their marital homes beyond commuting distance from the House of Commons, estrangement between husband and wife is a gradual but inevitable process, especially if the marriage has already reached a state of relative indifference. Even for London-based families, late-night sitting lethargy must take its toll on marital bliss.

In 1972 this toll was measurable. There were, at one point, reportedly forty-eight divorces pending in the House of Commons. The extraordinary rash of public ruptures owed its size to the suddenly liberal climate which followed the introduction of the new divorce laws. Divorce has been the ruin of many a political career. Even in the more favourable climate which now exists where divorce is concerned, the ambitious politician tries to avoid it. Connotations of scandal are never far where marriages break. One MP, himself divorced, says: 'If you want to get on in politics you don't change women in mid-stream.' One brilliant young Minister was allegedly sacked from the last Labour Cabinet for having a flagrant affair with his secretary. He has since been divorced. On the whole it is the back-benchers who allow themselves the luxury of divorce: though there was a time when this would cost a man his seat.

MPs have a very considerable reputation for womanising. There are alarming tales of lust and lechery in circulation about a number of prominent political figures.

There seems to be something in the make-up of politicians that brings on lechery at the slightest flicker of a woman's glance. One well-seasoned Member says that, 'All an attractive girl has to do, if she fancies her MP, is to go to the House and put in a green card for him, and he will come bounding out eagerly.'

Danger in the form of career-wrecking scandal may spice the adulterous dish for many an MP. But since this is abating, there is no corresponding slacking off of effort in Members' recruitment of girl-friends. Girls apparently meet MPs everywhere. On trains, in restaurants, certainly in the bars of the House and even on the street. Members of Parliament are highly trained opportunists — politicians must be — and it shows. A girl sitting in the Central Lobby of the House of Commons waiting for one MP can quite easily be accosted by another. I once picked up a Cabinet Minister in just this way.

Of course there are endless opportunities for the Members to meet women. Social occasions abound. As one Member remarked: 'Dolly birds are harder to find, but widows and divorcees are very plentiful.' And it would seem available. Women undoubtedly throw themselves at MPs. Members have the attraction of appearing to be powerful even if they are not. Christine Keeler, or one of her colleagues, was heard to observe that there is something exceptionally exciting about having sexual power over a powerful man.

The sublimation quotient of the letters MP would appear to be the equivalent of a Ferrari in the sexual stakes: women flock. Even the less attractive Members will find women more than eager to go out with them. This might only be once. As one girl put it, 'Dinner at the House of Commons sounds good — but when you've done it once . . .' MPs could do better for aphrodisiac dinners somewhere else, but clearly the House of Commons can act as bait.

The disadvantages, should they fall in love, are greater than for other categories of public person. The biggest snag in the way of true love between MPs and their mistresses is the old bogy of disaster in the form of divorce and public scandal. As Frances Stevenson found out, being a secret beloved is not all roses.

Clearly the most available woman in an MP's life is his secretary. A surprisingly large number of Members have affairs with their secretaries. One Member said: 'I was shocked when I found out what goes on in this place — especially some of the people!' Most men choose women employees that attract them from among the interviewees. MPs are no exception. David Steel, however, says: 'I always choose a girl who does not attract me — on purpose.'

The growing tendency seems to be for Members to divorce their wives and marry their secretaries. Douglas Jay, after a marriage of over twenty years' duration and at the age of 63 married his 29-year-old secretary. A number of other Members are doing the same.

Secretaries have the advantage over wives of being on the spot. They also have a working interest in the Member's daily life. They protect, guide, influence and serve. In return they get dinners bought for them and get taken to parties. According to one Member, some Members are far more frequently seen at parties with their secretaries than with their wives.

Members need mistresses in London if only because — as one put it: 'I like having someone to cuddle up to when I'm feeling low.' The conclusion is marriage — but at close range. However many times a Member marries, he will continue to chase girls. Politicians are vain men and constant conquest is gratifying. Even when the Member is impotent — as so many are reputed to be — the chase is as rewarding as ever. As one Member put it: 'The main pleasure is getting a girl to say yes.'

Marriage remains popular with MPs for a number of reasons. Although fewer MPs seem to be married than among the population as a whole, the requirement for marriage is greater. Apart from the obvious services performed by wives, there is the fact that some Members marry for fear of being thought homosexual.

In spite of some liberalising legislation, homosexuality still carries a bad social stigma. The last fact any politician would have known about himself would be this. It would be safer to be known as a philanderer, or to flaunt one's mistress than to be left open to the unspoken accusation of homosexuality. Yet several Members are homosexual. One MP told me: 'It's tragic the way they have to be so secretive.' He added: 'There is a sort of freemasonry in the House between the homosexual Members.'

The fear of being thought homosexual can also apply to married men. One young MP, interviewing for an assistant, received an application from a man who turned out to be a member of the Gay Liberation Front. During the course of his interview he asked the MP whether he would permit him to wear his Gay Lib button in the House. The MP was horror-stricken. 'Can you imagine,' he told me, 'how that would have made me look. I might as well wear one myself.'

There have been public cases of MPs prosecuted for alleged homosexual behaviour. Now the law at least permits homosexual love-making between consenting adults in private. But attitudes still make it necessary for homosexuals to hide their interests, and, worse, leave them open to blackmail. Only marriage is really respectable and even that has its dangers.

Temptation lies at every turn, some more dangerous than others. As one Labour Cabinet Minister once said to another: 'Do you think it would be safe for me to have an affair with someone in my constituency party?' The answer would have to be no. But politicians like excitement and revel in hairline danger. So many of them are open to instant ruin.

Naturally what Members do in their private time should be no one's business but their own. Unfortunately, once in public life there are the inevitable dangers accompanying any sort of eccentric behaviour. The puritanical attitudes of society make public figures particularly vulnerable to blackmail however innocent their indulgences. A number of leading and less well known political figures, for instance, participate in well organised orgies which my informant describes as high-minded depravities, concerned innocently enough with the wearing of plastic macs and leather brassières. Whenever any of these things became public knowledge there is disgrace — as with Lambton and Jellicoe. Fall is never far away for the sexually adventurous public figure.

The more wayward the politician the greater the number of vultures and jackals waiting in the wings. The planted security risk bombshell or the straight commercial bribe are all the more tempting for their availability. The unwary can easily be caught in a Profumo-type situation, so much so that at every scrap of scandal a shudder goes through Parliament. There but for the grace of God would go many a Member. For actors', shop-keepers' or dustmen's sexual habits only the *News of the World* would care. But politicians have to watch it. Maybe the time has passed when a Government could fall because of a Defence Minister's mistress, but one can never be too sure of the answers in politics.

As for the politician's wife, she must be circumspect in her behaviour too. Left behind to rot in the constituency, she has to avoid all temptation to sleep with the milkman. He might, after all, turn out to be a supporter from the other side.

SCRUTINY OF STATE

In January 1970 Brian Walden sponsored a Private Members
Bill on 'Right of Privacy'. In it he defined privacy as:

> 'The right of any person to be protected from intrusion
> upon himself, his home, his family, his relationships and
> communications with others, his property and his business
> affairs.'

Walden's Bill failed at its second reading. Yet among those
who would stand to gain particularly from its six main
principles were MPs themselves.

Most ordinary citizens are becoming increasingly at risk as
regards privacy, particularly of their business and financial
affairs. MPs have an additional hazard. They are public
figures. Not only are they recognisable but they are, unlike
actors, starlets, models and other categories of famous persons,
supposed to be respectable (even, nowadays to the point of
being expected to declare financial interests — by some
critics).

The Fame Factor

Some MPs are more famous than others. The degree of fame is
directly proportional to the amount of visual publicity given
to Members. Newspaper photographs are one hazard: but by
far the most potent method of becoming recognisable is to
appear on TV. Having done so, an MP is liable to be stared at,
told 'Haven't I seen you somewhere before?', 'I've seen you on
television', and 'Oh, you're so and so!'

According to Brian Walden, symptoms of being recognised are such things as, 'People turning round to look at you in restaurants, fidgeting and looking at you all the time. You become,' he says, 'suddenly aware of the tell-tale signs.' On another occasion Walden recalls kissing his girl-friend in the back of a taxi. 'When I got out to pay,' he said, 'the taxi-driver addressed me by my name.'

Luckily, Brian Walden is unmarried. There must be many married Members who have been similarly, though more keenly, embarrassed. Of course, taxi-drivers know everyone, and MPs in general are not such well-known names and faces that they need drive around with smoked-glass windows in their cars and coat collars up.

In their constituencies, MPs, particularly rural ones, can expect to be recognised pretty much everywhere they go. The same applies to their wives. Mrs. Ben Whittaker said she felt conscious that she should not 'Shout at the butcher or anything like that'. Mrs. Joy Pardoe says: 'Even the kind of car you have causes comment.' She describes one incident when the Pardoes' Hillman Imp came under comment. 'I shouldn't have thought,' said a constituent, 'that that was fast enough for you.' 'Of course,' says Mrs. Pardoe, 'they really meant classy enough.'

One of the disadvantages of having the family home in the constituency is that of having to keep up one's image all the time. Once I heard a Liberal constituency chairman say of a candidate: 'He wore jeans and the wife did too. It simply would not do here.' Someone with a more pin-stripe image was imported instead.

The MPs who live in their constituency leave most of the sweet behaviour to their wives. This can be something of a strain. A wife's behaviour is just as likely to reflect on the MP as his own. One MP's wife was stopped and breathalised on her way home from a party five years ago. Some of her husband's constituents still hold it against her.

Parliament, being in Westminster, MPs spent most of their week in London. At least there, there is a measure of anonymity. But London can be a very small town. Members are usually recognised by pressmen and there is a liberal sprinkling of them about central London any night of the week. Members out with girl-friends or business associates are unlikely to get off without being spotted at least once in any public place. No one is going to publish the gossip — for at least a few days — but it tends to become part of the pool of knowledge passed around among journalist and others. Fleet St. for example knew the details of the Marcia Williams-Walter Terry relationship many years before it became public knowledge in the early summer of 1974.

Some MPs are more sensitive than others to gossip. Harmless enough on the surface, it can damage a Member's chance of being taken seriously, especially by pressmen. To be respected, it seems, one must never fall from a Victorian standard of sobriety, chastity and dignity. If an MP wants to get drunk or have an orgy he had better do it behind sealed doors.

The Security Factor

Two of the points of Brian Walden's Privacy Bill, however, referred to the uncertainty that even sealed rooms are private. They referred to:

1. Spying, prying, watching or besetting;
2. The unauthorised overhearing or recording of spoken words.

He was particularly referring to bugging, tapping and other forms of spying on individuals. Perhaps he had in mind the experience of a number of Members of Parliament who have claimed to have suffered from this problem either persistently or sporadically. Walden himself claims that 'I was certainly followed once'.

On November 17th, 1966, Roy Jenkins, then Home Secretary, came under attack in the House. Several Labour MPs and one or two Conservative Members were suspicious that confidential telephone conversations were being listened to. One MP, David Ensor, told a *Sunday Express* reporter, 'It is a nice state of affairs when an MP feels he cannot ring up even a constituent without a suspicion in his mind that the conversation is being listened to.'

The same *Express* reporter wrote, 'At least one back-bencher believes that his correspondence is being tampered with.' Such was the anxiety of MPs that Mr. Wilson, who could never resist a crisis of confidence, stepped in to answer the question directed at Mr. Jenkins. 'MPs were,' he said, 'a special case. Their telephones had not been tapped since Labour took office in 1964.'

But someone somewhere was busy giving MPs uneasy thoughts. One MP said: 'Until the business is cleared up I shall carry on using public phone boxes, for my confidential calls because I believe my own phone is tapped.'

Russell Kerr said in the House, following Mr. Wilson's denial, that many MPs believed rightly or wrongly that their telephones had been tapped. Tactfully, perhaps too tactfully, he said, 'While the House would acquit you of any knowledge of or complicity in this, will you consult the Home Secretary and the Paymaster General [George Wigg] to make sure that some of our security people are not undertaking free enterprise of a rather smelly kind on this issue.'

The question was now, as it still is: if not the authorities, then who was listening on such a large and often clumsy scale to the telephone calls of MPs? Sir Tufton Beamish claimed at this time that 'the tapping and taping' of private telephone conversations without the knowledge of the Post Office and without authority was much worse than anybody imagined. Sir Tufton said that, before replacing the receiver, he had actually heard a recording of his conversation played back after he had finished speaking.

To all this the Prime Minister gave no categorical denial and the question still remains. Are MPs telephones tapped? Is their mail opened, and if so by whom? For the sake of respectability, the argument has been moved to one about unauthorised tapping. But there are still MPs who think that authorised tapping goes on. The authorisation for tapping of a telephone is theoretically given by the Home Secretary. The process then is fairly simple: a tap is set up from a special GPO Exchange.

Telephones are officially tapped for all kinds of purposes from breaking up of criminal organisations to catching spies. The most disturbing aspect of telephone tapping and other forms of scrutiny is that the innocent can be spied upon as well as the guilty. One of the problems with political telephone tapping is this guilt by association. Telephone tapping of a Member's phone can occur because he is the link in a chain between an associate and a so-called security risk. The same can apply to a person telephoning an MP who happens to be under scrutiny. If the conversation appears to be of interest to the scrutinisers, the MP's caller also gets a tap. Telephone tapping is as catching as venereal disease.

'Security risk' is the title applied to anyone whose indiscretions could land them in a blackmail situation likely to be dangerous to the security of the State. Politicians, whether in Parliament or otherwise, are fair game in, that case, for official suspicions. They are strangely adept at being led astray. They wander inadvertently in a nebulous half world of crime, espionage, fraud, corruption and fellow-travelling. This can have its lighter side. John Pardoe, who shared an office with Lord Beaumont in Victoria Street, says that two young Liberals free-lancing in research and journalism had desks there also. 'We began to suspect,' he says, 'that our telephones were tapped, and it was obvious why.' It was hiliarious to say the least that Lord Beaumont should be considered in any way a danger to the State. The cause of the tapping was the two young Liberals. 'They moved,' said an amused Pardoe, 'in what I would call narco-revolutionary circles. I cannot imagine,' he laughed, 'a more seditious combination than these two.'

If the authorities do tap telephones on as large a scale as many political people believe, it is more on the left than on the right. Brian Walden says: 'It is associations with Moscow they are watching for.' Reds under beds again. But mostly with their feet sticking out. It is a clever operator indeed who behaves like a left-winger and gets away with any 'security leaks' for long. The apparently middle of the road or right wing 'crypto' is the more dangerous in real security terms. Perhaps this is why, as one authoritive source told me, 'All candidates and MPs are given a routine check from time to time.' The check includes telephone-tapping and tailing. Other forms of scrutiny such as investigation of a politician's financial affairs — how much have they got in the bank and where does it come from — and opening of mail can occur if there seem to be any 'suspicious circumstance'.

An engaging attribute of politicians, especially those on the left who according to my source 'come in for almost continuous scrutiny', is that they rarely hide their true political attitudes. They have to communicate their politics and are far too open to be successful agents. Yet, according to this source, some left-wing MPs are followed about all the time.

Clearly being a politician is a naked business. But however sinister the apparent invasion of their privacy may be, not all MPs are willing that it should stop. An all-party committee of Privy Councillors said in 1957 that MPs should be treated no differently from members of the public. And Hugh Fraser asked in the House during the November 1966 row over tapping, why MPs should be excluded from a process which was considered necessary 'for the protection of national security and the prevention of crime.'

The unfortunate part about tapping and other forms of scrutiny is that even where they are suspected by the victim they cannot be proved, and if the authorities deny all knowledge they are not necessarily telling the truth. But it is not only official sources which tap telephones. Perhaps the great clumsiness that enables so many of the victims of tapping to detect eavesdroppers all to easily, is an indication that amateurs are at work.

Amateur telephone-tapping and other forms of eavesdropping are available at a fairly low fee in London. For one hundred pounds the police can obtain the services of freelance telephone tappers — usually men who have been in prison at sometime or other or who have some similar relationship with the police. If the police can do it, why not anyone? Iron curtain countries go in for amateur eavesdropping on a large scale.

MPs, particularly those on the left-wing, and also any political activist showing leftish sentiments might make useful helpers. By spying on them, foreign powers can learn to what extent their sympathies are likely to turn into active support. Also, evidence for future blackmail can be compiled.

One of the current spy stories concerning MPs involves alleged collaboration between South African BOSS (Bureau of State Security) agents in this country and our own security forces. James Wellbeloved raised the question in the Commons, but currently he and the National Council of Civil Liberties are 'not saying much for the time being'. The allegation involves telephone tapping, bugging and spying on individuals likely to oppose the régime in South Africa. The people involved include several MPs. One of these, Andrew Faulds, a dedicated opponent of apartheid, has often complained privately of telephone tapping. Once he said: 'I know someone was in my flat while I was away. I never smoke and I could smell tobacco on the mouthpiece of the telephone.' South African tobacco perhaps?

MPs rarely complain in the House about their suspicions of being under scrutiny. Those who do complain to their colleagues are often considered 'paranoid' or 'over-estimating their own importance'. Asked about this aspect of their own privacy, some MPs go slitty-eyed and play down their responses. If tapping and other forms of privacy invasion are practised on politicians more than other people and by the authorities to boot, the MPs, says one Member, 'Have only themselves to blame for not exposing this grey area.'

The Protection Factor

If security can operate to invade a Member's privacy it can also operate to protect him. The House of Commons is currently more well guarded than usual due to the dangers from Irish terrorists. The usual brigade of policemen whose tedious task it is to do Parliamentary duty has strengthened. The familiar faces of constables and sergeants who have patrolled the entrances and lobbies for years are now almost lost among a sea of newer ones. But security is not consistently operated for all that. 'Some days,' says David Steel, 'they won't even let the MPs in.' On other days, I have myself sailed past into the inner sanctum with a careless wave.

Security in the House of Commons has its objectionable side. In theory there is no earthly reason why taxpayers should not go anywhere they please in the House, accompanied or otherwise, apart from the possible chaos they might cause. The police act, in fact, like doormen at a rather exclusive club, keeping the rabble out and making them well aware of their 'place'.

Police can, however, be of considerable service in protecting MPs. Andrew Bowden is one MP who has asked for police protection in his own constituency following threats made to his family and himself by political extremists.

Since the first of the political bombings in Britain — that of Robert Carr, then Secretary of State for Employment, whose home was blasted by the so-called Angry Brigade — increased hazards from letter bombs, and attacks on government buildings have meant that politicians are now under closer protection than at any time past. Even Liberal candidates were threatened with a vague promise of letter bombs during the February 1974 Election. Without pattern or prediction anyone in the public eye is likely to get at least a threat as anyone with a grievance gets in on the act.

Security and protection go hand in hand with extensive intelligence. It is reasonable, therefore, to assume that the greater the protection of politicians or society require from unknown enemies, the greater the loss of privacy for all concerned. Politics is the centre of change and power. Where these forces become more violently held they will be more violently attacked: and through violence, protection must increase. We can therefore expect that while current trends continue the privacy of political people, Members of Parliament included, will continue to be eroded through the apparently decent medium of the State. Fame and recognition may be one aspect of public life but they are mere trivia of inconvenience, compared with the seriously growing situation of that invasion of privacy which has national or personal security as its excuse. Members of Parliament who suspect that their telephones are being tapped owe it to the rest of us to make every effort to isolate the cause of the violation. If anyone can protect privacy, even their own, it can only be the MPs.

Part V

IN CONCLUSION

A *Punch* cartoon of 1832 showing two politicians at the hustings was captioned *Rival Rogues*: Commisioner Punch: 'Gentlemen, your candour is charming. Not a pin to choose between you. You both deserve penal servitude [aside] and I hope — some day — you get it!' Sharp stuff — and with a familiar ring. Voters, as was reported in the introductory sections of this book, are still having trouble telling the difference between their politicians.

But there are more important parallels between the year of the cartoon and the present period: 1832 was the year of the Second Reform Bill. Throughout the next fifty years, until the extension of the franchise to include almost every adult male in the country, Electoral and Parliamentary reform were recurrently topical. And so they are today. But this time they do not concern the franchise itself but the accuracy of representation and the effectiveness of Parliament to represent — not merely classes of society, but all the multifarious and volatile needs of a society undergoing rapid restructuring and historic change.

Throughout the preceding chapters the principle discussion has centred upon the difficulty of doing the job that is in some way willed, unwritten and unspoken in the constitution of Britain.

That task is to represent, but as we have seen, with the best will in the world, the task is only a quarter effected because the system itself defies the principle it exists to serve. If more evidence was needed, the results of the February General Election in 1974 provided the final case for a radical reform in the Parliamentary system. After years of apathy and political disinterest, of the acceptance of the impassivity of the two-party system this freaky, pattern-breaking election with its record number of minority candidates, the larger number of votes cast for them and the indefinite nature of the result were like a springtime for reform. The collective will for a change, which was more than a swap arrangement between two parties themselves confined within the straitjacket of the system, had at last expressed itself.

In this context the remarks made by eminent Parliamentarians a century and a half ago are especially pertinent. As early as April 1822 Lord John Russell said in the House of Commons: 'The votes of the House of Commons no longer imply the general assent of the realm; they no longer carry with them the sympathies and understandings of the nation.' Thomas Babington Macaulay, speaking in the debate on the first Reform Bill on March 2nd, 1831, said: 'Turn where we may, within, around, the voice of great events is proclaiming to us, Reform, that you may preserve.'

The survival of Parliamentary democracy in Britain is one issue confronted each time the need for reform arises. But the purpose of the reform is improvement of the system, bringing it closer to its ideal. The pressure for reforms of many kinds which will enable Members of Parliament to carry out their traditional function is now increasing. At every stage in the process of selecting and electing MPs, and then within the House itself changes are being invited.

Electoral reform of some kind is fundamental to the achievement of a more accurate reflection of political viewpoint amongst the voters. But there are other aspects. Such oddities as the fact that so many voters have no idea either how to vote or what their vote signifies, could easily be corrected by adding a half-hour class on voting once a year to the curriculum of the school-leaver, or even by circulating voters with simple instructions on voting procedures at the taxpayers' expense once every five years or so.

But once elected, by whatever system, the Members should have their working and their private lives eased by such simple reforms as a regularisation of Parliamentary hours, the provision of full-time paid assistants, proper office facilities, and proper and adequate payment for the work they do. These are physical rather than psychological changes but they would — as will the new Parliamentary building, if it is ever built — increase the physical ability of MPs to do their work.

MPs currently try to work under conditions, with such facilities and hours and for pay related to that work which few, if any, of the Trade Union Mmbers would accept as fair for any working man. Members whose experience is of management would also be unlikely to tolerate such conditions at a normal place of work.

But even if these streamlining changes were to come into effect immediately they would probably only serve to highlight the fact that however such changes would facilitate the flow of help and information between the Member and his constituents; however they would perhaps improve his general level of knowledge through the availability of better managed time, the Member is still relatively powerless against Government in the major work area of legislation.

It was Edward DuCann who, during a TV debate on Parliamentary Reform, said: 'The power of the Executive is increasing and I believe that Parliament has a historic duty to contain it.' But the ability to contain the encroachment of Executive power is lacking — or if present at all, is tempered by the silken cords of the Whipping system and its 'appeals to party loyalty'.

The area of the struggle has moved from the ambit of the individual MP to the camp of party. Only through increased representation of parties in the House and the eventual acceptance of a degree of flexibility in their voting patterns can the power of the Executive be in any way contained. The minority Government of 1974 was a pointer to the ways in which Parliament might reorientate itself among the greater freedoms of the balance of power. But, once again, only an acceptance by Government of its vulnerability and the acceptance of parties that legislative defeats in division were not a signal for the Government to fall, could enable the reorientation to begin.

The possibility that legislation might be initiated in the

House on a larger scale by Private Members or by Opposition parties also has to be considered. But this possibility raises a further major difficulty over the accessibility of expert information. It is enshrined in the system that only the Government and its officers have access to the nations books and the people who keep them, i.e. Whitehall. It is in this area of information that, in a modern state, the dangers of an inadequately informed Parliament are most apparent. Members themselves are feeling an increasing need to be properly informed and, as was discussed in Part II, Chapter 1, feel that one solution is a greater specialisation and division of labour amongst Members.

There is clearly a very great need for Members to have both the time and the facility to increase their specialist knowledge but also to have the machinery available to put it to use in terms of producing wise legislation; and also to keep pace with and check the *fait accompli* of Government — those administrative decisions whose only chance of being checked is during Question Time or through the indefatigable efforts of individual MPs.

As David Howell remarked: 'It is in this crucial but twilight central area of secretariats and task forces and working groups and confidential reports — where the final strategic decisions of public policy often come to be settled — that skilled probing by Parliamentary committees could illuminate and ventilate in a way that party oppositions cannot.'

In a sense Howell put his finger on the ace: the executive and the party are twin tyrants standing against the power of MPs.

Only time will tell which are the stronger.

THE BRITISH GENIUS
Peter Grosvenor and James McMillan

'As to this country it is sunk, never to rise again. We have dwindled into an insignificant island. We have neither wisdom nor virtue left'

Thus Horace Walpole, nearly two centuries ago; and people have increasingly echoed his sentiments ever since.

Revised and updated for this paperback publication, THE BRITISH GENIUS comes as something of a corrective, a work of reference that stands as the first one-volume guide to British achievements in every walk of life in this century. Not so much an anatomy of Britain as a physiology – a look at how the people of Britain have contributed so much in so many fields of progress. There are pen-portraits of most of the leading artistic figures; there are lists of the principal British inventions; there is a mass of fascinating statistics; there is a good deal of hitherto unpublished material.

The whole adds up to a book that will stimulate and entertain a large readership.

'What a good book this is' – *Sunday Times*

'Reach out for this book, open it at any chapter you like and delight in getting back your pride in the genius of the British ... This is a book worth having on the bookshelf, once to read it very thoroughly, and after that for constant reference' – Lord Robens, *The Director*

IN THE COUNTRY
Kenneth Allsop

'A lush account of a year in the Hardy country ... In an age when a single earth-moving machine can remove a thousand years of history in an hour, you need a Kenneth Allsop's eye, ear and pen' – *Sunday Times*

'Ideal fireside reading for anybody who likes to be reminded that there is a wider and more rewarding world than the one we have tried to make' – *The Scotsman*

'Above all he writes with joy. And his triumph is to transmit that joy to the reader, opening tired old townie eyes to new or long-forgotten horizons, rekindling old pleasures, and, best of all, stirring enthusiasms that seemed long since dead. If you can't live in the country yourself, the next best thing is to have Mr. Allsop do it for you by proxy' – (Peter Tinniswood in the) *Western Mail*

CHANGING DIRECTIONS: THE FINDINGS OF THE INDEPENDENT COMMISSION ON TRANSPORT

Are we in charge of transport, or is transport taking charge of us?

Already it is having a frightening effect on our quality of life. There is hardly a person in the country who is not often appalled by the sights and sounds and smells that emanate from most forms of transport; and there are no fewer who come close to impatience with the delays, the inflexibilities, the seeming wastefulness that result from the increase in traffic of all forms.

As transport problems increase, so the need for solutions becomes more urgent. Momentous decisions must soon be taken, and important questions – concerning such matters as mobility, resources, social justice, safety, amenity, efficiency and noise – will soon be asked.

Last year Bishop Hugh Montefiore set up a commission to investigate Britain's transport, with Stephen Plowden as Executive Secretary. This is the report of that commission, written for the ordinary reader, based on expert knowledge and opinion. An attempt is made to paint the whole picture, to look at the problem in the round. And the result is a book that everyone should look at.

CORONET BOOKS

CORONET NON-FICTION

All these books are available at your bookshop or newsagent, or can be ordered direct from the publisher. Just tick the titles you want and fill in the form below.

....

CORONET BOOKS, P.O. Box 11, Falmouth, Cornwall.
Please send cheque or postal order. No currency, and allow the following for postage and packing:
1 book—10p, 2 books—15p, 3 books—20p, 4–5 books—25p, 6–9 books—4p per copy, 10–15 books—2½p per copy, 16–30 books—2p per copy, over 30 books free within the U.K.
Overseas – please allow 10p for the first book and 5p per copy for each additional book.

Name ....

Address ....

....

....